GRACE GIFFORD PLUNKETT
AND IRISH FREEDOM

Portrait of Grace Plunkett by Seán O'Sullivan

GRACE GIFFORD PLUNKETT AND IRISH FREEDOM

Tragic Bride of 1916

MARIE O'NEILL

IRISH ACADEMIC PRESS

DUBLIN • PORTLAND, OR

First published in 2000 by
IRISH ACADEMIC PRESS
44, Northumberland Road,
Dublin 4, Ireland

and in the United States of America by
IRISH ACADEMIC PRESS
c/o ISBS, 5804 NE Hassalo Street,
Portland, OR 97213 3644

Website: www.iap.ie

British Library Cataloguing in Publication Data
O'Neill, Marie
    Grace Gifford Plunkett and Irish Freedom: tragic bride of 1916
    1. Plunkett, Grace Gifford   2. Plunkett, Joseph M., 1887–1916 –
    Marriage   3. Revolutionaries' spouses – Ireland – Biography
    4. Women revolutionaries – Ireland – Biography
    5. Ireland – History – Easter Rising, 1916
    I. Title
    941.5'082'092

    ISBN 0-7165-2666-2 (cloth),
        0-7165-2713-8 (paper)

Library of Congress Cataloging-in-Publication Data
O'Neill, Marie
    Grace Gifford Plunkett and Irish Freedom : tragic bride of 1916 /
by Marie O'Neill.
        p.   cm. — (Women in Irish history)
    Includes bibliographical references and index.
    ISBN 0-7165-2666-2.   —ISBN 0-7165-2713-8 (pbk.)
    1. Plunkett, Grace Gifford, 1888–1955.   2. Ireland—History—
Easter Rising, 1916 Biography.   3. Plunkett, Joseph Mary,
1887–1916—Marriage.   4. Revolutionaries' spouses—Ireland
Biography.   5. Women revolutionaries—Ireland Biography.
6. Authors' spouses—Ireland biography.   7. Women artists—Ireland—
Biography.   I. Title.   II. Series.
DA965.P59064   1999   941.5082'1—dc21
[B]   99-36022

Typeset by Regent Typesetting, London
Printed by Creative Print and Design (Wales) Ltd,
Ebbw Vale

Contents

List of Illustrations

Foreword

GRACE GIFFORD PLUNKETT has received her place in Irish history as the woman who married the poet, Joseph Mary Plunkett, one of the leaders of the 1916 Easter Rising in Dublin, a few hours before his execution. Within a year she was an icon and, throughout a long widowhood, she remained, in the words of her biographer, Marie O'Neill, 'a powerful symbolic figure of the republican ideal for which her husband had given his life'. In many respects it was an empty symbol, a few stark minutes frozen in time, located in the prison chapel of Kilmainham jail, a small poignant episode in the story of Kilmainham jail, through whose gates passed the most famous political prisoners of Irish history: Charles Stewart Parnell to freedom in 1882, and the leaders of the 1916 Rising to their execution in the yard outside the prison cells. Grace Gifford was twenty-eight years of age when she married Joseph Mary Plunkett, and she lived alone for a further thirty-nine years, her lively, sociable personality and her witty, mischievous cartoons concealing her innermost feelings of sorrow, disappointment and ultimately of solitariness.

Marie O'Neill has rescued Grace Gifford from the passivity of the tableau set eternally in Kilmainham prison chapel. A skilled biographer, Marie O'Neill found the building blocks which enabled her to present Grace Gifford in a coherent, lucid narrative that gives the reader a sense of who Grace Gifford was, where she came from in the context of family, and what she became after her brief, sorrowful marriage ceremony. Marie O'Neill, with historical and legal training, has for many years immersed herself in the revolutionary period that spans the activities of the Ladies Land League in the early 1880s through the aftermath of the 1916 Easter Rising. Her biography of Jenny Wyse Power was a noteworthy achievement which revealed her talents as a biographer and researcher.

Undertaking a life of Grace Gifford Plunkett was a challenging task and the search for evidence was rewarded by the amount that awaited her in the collections of the National Library of Ireland and the Military History Bureau. The value of her interviews with members of the Gifford and Plunkett families is apparent in the delicacy and skill with which Marie O'Neill deals with the key issues in Grace Gifford's life such as her relationship with her parents and with Joseph Plunkett's mother and with Grace's pregnancy and miscarriage.

The profile of Grace Gifford Plunkett that emerges from Marie O'Neill's biography is that of a strong independent woman whose artistic talent manifested itself in satirical cartoons of a political and topical nature. She came from a unionist, upper-class family and from a mixed marriage in which the daughters were educated in their mother's religion, Church of Ireland, and the sons in that of their father, Roman Catholicism. In the large family of twelve children, the Gifford girls offer a gender study of much interest. They chose vigorous, exciting careers that women's education and political activities of a nationalist and republican flavour offered. Grace converted to Catholicism as her acquaintanceship with Joe Plunkett deepened into love. Marie O'Neill never loses her way in the thickets of family history. She adroitly gives tantalising cameos of Grace's parents and of her sisters, Sydney and Muriel in particular, yet she allows Grace and her life to occupy the central space in the story of this unusual family of Dublin girls at the turn of the century.

One of the singular attractions of Grace Gifford's biography is the intimate knowledge of Dublin that Marie O'Neill exhibits in the details of where Grace lived after the execution of her husband. It was a Dublin of small rented flats and single rooms, the precarious lot of widows and single women in the first decades of the Free State. Grace received a civil list pension when Eamon de Valera and Fianna Fail came into government in 1932, but for many years her commercial and theatrical cartoons were her sole means of livelihood. Her work as a humorist and cartoonist is increasing in recognition as writers and critics examine perspectives of the period other than politics.

Grace Gifford Plunkett died suddenly and alone in her apartment at 52 South Richmond Street on 13 December 1955. Her funeral was accorded full military honours and was attended by the President, Sean T. O'Kelly, his wife Phyllis, by Eamon de Valera and by her sisters and relatives. Donagh MacDonagh, her nephew, recalled how she has passed into ballads and thus entered what he describes as 'the most secure of all National Pantheons, the world of the ballad'.

'I loved Joe Plunkett and he loved me
He gave his life to set Ireland free.'

Marie O'Neill's biography which she has subtitled 'Tragic Bride of 1916' is absorbing reading-matter. She has infused her researches with a charm of style which illuminates the central character and her background. She has demonstrated through following the life-story of Grace Gifford Plunkett how young women, in the words of one of Grace's contemporaries, Máire Comerford, 'took fire' from 1916 Rising and were changed by the experience. This biography of Grace Gifford Plunkett invites reflection on an extraordinary generation of Irish women and men who risked everything they held dear for an ideal of political freedom.

Margaret MacCurtain
Dublin, June 1999

Mrs J. Plunkett 1916

Acknowledgements

WHEN I began to research the life of Grace Plunkett (née Gifford), she had been dead for forty years. It was difficult to find people who knew her well but fortunately I did find several who shared their recollections with me. Without their help, this book could not have been written.

Special mention must be made of Grace's niece, Maeve Donnelly, to whom my thanks alas come posthumously. Despite her own failing health, she allowed me to interview her and showed me her souvenirs of Grace. Both Maeve and her mother, Nellie, enjoyed a close and loving relationship with Grace which lasted until Grace's death in 1955. Maeve died in December 1997.

Blanaid O'Brolchain, niece of Joseph Mary Plunkett, also gave me special help. Her mother, Geraldine Dillon (née Plunkett) had been very close to her famous brother and frequently wrote about him during her long life. Geraldine died in 1985 and Blanaid died in 1998.

My greatest debt is to Ann Burke. She knew Grace well from early childhood as her parents, John L. Burke and his wife, were close friends of Grace who was a frequent visitor to their home in Rathgar. Ann talked to me many times about Grace and showed me the drawings and other memorabilia of Grace which her father had acquired over many years and also some letters Grace had written to him. Ann also lent me the sketch of Grace in her youth by William Orpen which is reproduced on the jacket of this book.

Special thanks must also go to the late Cathal Gannon and his son Charles. Cathal knew Grace well in her middle years and wrote his memories of her which he allowed me to see. These provided many interesting details which I would not have known without his help.

The staff of the National Library were, as always, courteous and helpful. Special thanks must go to Colette O'Daly, librarian for Prints and Drawings, who helped me in finding illustrations. Noel Kissane of the Manuscripts Department also gave me substantial assistance. The staff of the Gilbert Library also helped me as did Professor John Turpin of the National College of Art and Design and the librarian there, Edward Murphy. Pat Cooke, curator of the Kilmainham Prison Museum and several members of his staff also assisted me, in particular Niamh O'Sullivan, Elizabeth Carey and Brenda Kenny. Brenda gave me a private tour of the former jail and showed me several mementoes of Grace which were on loan there for the 'Guns and Chiffon' exhibition. She also showed me the mementoes of Joseph Mary Plunkett which had been donated or left to the Museum. Sinead McCoole, the biographer of Hazel Lavery, also deserves my thanks.

Commandants Peter Young and Victor Lang of the Army Archives were helpful in obtaining information from records about Grace's imprisonment during the Civil War. Oliver Snoddy was patient and kind in advising me and sharing his detailed knowledge of the period.

My thanks also go to the following who helped in various ways: Sheil Carden, Monica Henchy, Vivienne Igoe, Mary King, Professor Donal MacCartney, Ciaran McGonigal, Mary Mitchell and her staff in the Dalkey Public Library, Professor Kevin B. Nowlan, Eithne O'Byrne, Nellie O'Cleirigh, Anne O'Connor of Alexandra College, Gregory O'Connor of the National Archives, the late Caitlin O'Neill, Stephen Plunkett, Moya Russell, Joanna Shacklock of the Slade School of Art and Eda Ni Tuama of the Royal Irish Academy.

Permission to reproduce Grace's cartoons and sketches was given by the late Maeve Donnelly and confirmed by her executors. The copy of the portrait of Grace by Sean O'Sullivan was supplied by the National Gallery of Ireland and permission to reproduce it was kindly given by Terry Myler. The photograph of Grace taken in 1916 for a Chicago newspaper is reproduced courtesy of the Kilmainham Jail Museum. Dr. Pat Wallace, Director of the National Museum of Ireland kindly gave permission to reproduce the 1916 Proclamation of the Republic and the National Library of Ireland allowed me to reproduce material in its collections. David Sheehy, Archivist to the Archdiocese of Dublin, was helpful in obtaining information from the records there. Special thanks must also go to Gifford Lewis who allowed me to quote from *The Years Flew By*, the recollections of Grace's sister Sydney Gifford Czira, a valuable source for the early life of the family.

It has been a pleasure to work with Linda Longmore of Irish Academic Press and the editor there, Stephanie Dagg, both of whom were helpful in every way. I am grateful to Professor Margaret MacCurtain for agreeing to write the foreword. To Hazel Sheil who typed the manuscript with patience and interest, my warmest thanks are due. To my family and friends, who listened to my constant talk about my subject and the dramatic times through which she lived, I am obliged for encouragement and support throughout the project.

Marie O'Neill,
August, 1999

Introduction

THE HISTORY of Ireland in the first two decades of the twentieth century is a dramatic story. The armed rising which erupted in Dublin at Easter 1916 came as a surprise to the world outside but the signs that it would happen were known to many within Ireland. At the beginning of the century Ireland appeared to be relatively peaceful. The country had been ruled from Westminster since the Act of Union in 1800. In the British House of Commons there were about one hundred members who represented Irish constituencies. The Vice-Regal Lodge in the Phoenix Park (now Aras an Uachtarain) was the home of the Viceroy, the representative of the British Sovereign in Ireland. Dublin Castle was the seat of power where the Chief Secretary and his staff administered the daily routine of government. Voting rights had been extended in both Britain and Ireland in the second half of the nineteenth century. Voting by secret ballot had been introduced after 1872. In Ireland this measure was very important because it relieved voters of pressure by landlords and employers to vote according to their dictates. The struggle to obtain Home Rule – i.e. a separate Irish parliament – started in 1870 and from 1900 was continued by the Irish Nationalist party in the House of Commons under the leadership of John Redmond, the member for Waterford. Eventually a Home Rule Act was passed into law in May 1914 but its operation was suspended when the First World War started in August of that year.

A new voice in Irish politics, that of Arthur Griffith, emerged in the year 1904 with the publication of *The Resurrection of Hungary*. A Dublin man, who worked as a printer and later as a journalist, Griffith admired the success of Hungary in achieving a dual monarchy with Austria. He thought a similiar relationship between Britain and Ireland might be mutually acceptable. Griffith promoted a policy of self-reliance in both politics and economics. Having little faith in the prospect of the Irish members of parliament achieving Home Rule, he urged them to withdraw from Westminster, meet in Dublin and establish an Irish Government. Such action, he believed, would make British rule impossible and bring about a peaceful revolution. Griffith promoted, his policies through his newspaper the *United Irishman* and, from 1906 onwards *Sinn Féin*. Although the idea of a dual monarchy had little appeal for Irish nationalists, in time Griffith became an important political leader. After 1916, his Sinn Féin organisation expanded dramatically and in 1917 it adopted a republican constitution aimed at international recognition of Ireland as an independent state.

Concurrent with the struggle for political independence, a cultural renaissance known as the Celtic Revival was taking place. The Gaelic League, founded in 1893 by Douglas Hyde, Eoin MacNeill and others, led the way. Branches formed all over the country taught the Irish language and Irish history to a new generation of young men and women. Irish music and dancing provided entertainment and the league fostered a pleasant social side to its serious work.

The movement to obtain votes for women was becoming more vigorous. It started as a gentle campaign in 1876 when the Quaker leader, Anna Haslam, founded the Dublin Women's Suffrage Association. This grew into a larger body, the Irishwomen's Suffrage and Local Government Association, which led a country-wide campaign. Women achieved a role in local government with the passing of the Local Government of Ireland Act in 1898. However the aim of achieving votes for members of parliament met with strong resistance and it became obvious to a younger generation that more militant tactics were needed. In 1908, Hanna Sheehy Skeffington and Margaret Cousins founded a new group, the Irish Women's Franchise League, which was prepared to use more forceful tactics.

Another group of women, the Daughters of Erin, (Inghinidhe na hEireann) had been founded in Dublin in the year 1900. This was a separatist organisation, led by Maud Gonne, which aimed at the complete independence of Ireland. The group promoted Gaelic culture, organising free classes which taught Irish, history and music. Irish manufacturers were supported. Theatrical entertainments were arranged in the Ancient Concert Rooms in Brunswick Street, Dublin (now Pearse Street). The poet William Butler Yeats wrote his play *Kathleen Ni Houlihan* for the group. Maud Gonne played the leading role in its first production with great success. Among those who worked actively with the group were Jennie Wyse Power, the patriot and feminist, Anna Johnson who wrote under the pen name of Ethna Carbery, Maíre Quinn and Sinead Flanagan who later married Eamon de Valera. Among those who took part in theatrical productions were Mary Walker (Maire Ni Shiubhlaigh) and the sisters Sara Allgood and Maire O'Neill, all of whom later became well-known actresses.

The role of Augusta Lady Gregory in promoting new departures in the theatre is well-known. She became the friend and patron of William Butler Yeats and together they founded the Irish Literary Theatre which preceded the famous Abbey Theatre in Dublin. Plays by Lady Gregory, William Butler Yeats, John Millington Synge and Edward Martyn were staged in the early years. There was a great flowering of Irish literary talent in this period. Many wrote poetry, including the future revolutionary leaders Patrick Pearse, Thomas MacDonagh and Joseph Mary Plunkett. George Russell (known by his pen-name Æ) worked with Sir Horace Plunkett to promote co-operation in farming. In his spare time he painted and wrote poetry. Interest in art was also increasing at this time. Hugh Lane, the Cork-born critic and collector who became a very successful dealer in London, led the way. After meeting W.B. Yeats at the home of his aunt Lady Gregory he began to take an interest in the Irish art scene. He became the driving force in the attempt to found a new Gallery of Modern Art in Dublin. He lent a fine collection of his paintings to a temporary Municipal Gallery in Harcourt Street. He offered to make the loan into a gift if a new permanent gallery was provided.

Dublin was a vibrant city in the early years of the century. The political structures were not as secure as they seemed and old values were being challenged in various ways. Growing up in the period were the poet and future revolutionary leader, Joseph Mary Plunkett and Grace Gifford, who became a talented artist. This book tells the story of how they met and fell in love, of how they married in tragic circumstances and of how Grace the widow passed the rest of her life. Their generation has now passed away and many know little or nothing about them. My aim has been to recall their story and place them in the turbulent period through which they lived.

Marie O'Neill
June 1999

POBLACHT NA H EIREANN.

THE PROVISIONAL GOVERNMENT

OF THE

IRISH REPUBLIC

TO THE PEOPLE OF IRELAND.

IRISHMEN AND IRISHWOMEN: In the name of God and of the dead generations from which she receives her old tradition of nationhood, Ireland, through us, summons her children to her flag and strikes for her freedom.

Having organised and trained her manhood through her secret revolutionary organisation, the Irish Republican Brotherhood, and through her open military organisations, the Irish Volunteers and the Irish Citizen Army, having patiently perfected her discipline, having resolutely waited for the right moment to reveal itself, she now seizes that moment, and, supported by her exiled children in America and by gallant allies in Europe, but relying in the first on her own strength, she strikes in full confidence of victory.

We declare the right of the people of Ireland to the ownership of Ireland, and to the unfettered control of Irish destinies, to be sovereign and indefeasible. The long usurpation of that right by a foreign people and government has not extinguished the right, nor can it ever be extinguished except by the destruction of the Irish people. In every generation the Irish people have asserted their right to national freedom and sovereignty: six times during the past three hundred years they have asserted it in arms. Standing on that fundamental right and again asserting it in arms in the face of the world, we hereby proclaim the Irish Republic as a Sovereign Independent State, and we pledge our lives and the lives of our comrades-in-arms to the cause of its freedom, of its welfare, and of its exaltation among the nations.

The Irish Republic is entitled to, and hereby claims, the allegiance of every Irishman and Irishwoman. The Republic guarantees religious and civil liberty, equal rights and equal opportunities to all its citizens, and declares its resolve to pursue the happiness and prosperity of the whole nation and of all its parts, cherishing all the children of the nation equally, and oblivious of the differences carefully fostered by an alien government, which have divided a minority from the majority in the past.

Until our arms have brought the opportune moment for the establishment of a permanent National Government, representative of the whole people of Ireland and elected by the suffrages of all her men and women, the Provisional Government, hereby constituted, will administer the civil and military affairs of the Republic in trust for the people.

We place the cause of the Irish Republic under the protection of the Most High God, Whose blessing we invoke upon our arms, and we pray that no one who serves that cause will dishonour it by cowardice, inhumanity, or rapine. In this supreme hour the Irish nation must, by its valour and discipline and by the readiness of its children to sacrifice themselves for the common good, prove itself worthy of the august destiny to which it is called.

Signed on Behalf of the Provisional Government,

THOMAS J. CLARKE,
SEAN Mac DIARMADA,   THOMAS MacDONAGH,
P. H. PEARSE,   EAMONN CEANNT,
JAM. CONNOLLY.   JOSEPH PLUNKETT.

CHAPTER ONE

Beginnings

THE NAME of Grace Gifford Plunkett first came to the knowledge of the general public in dramatic circumstances after the Easter Rising in Dublin, 1916. Grace was engaged to marry Joseph Mary Plunkett, one of the military leaders of the Rising. He was also one of the signatories of the Proclamation of the Republic. Despite serious illness at the time, Plunkett was one of the group that occupied the General Post Office. They held the building for six days before surrender. Within a short time, the British forces in Dublin arrested the leaders. Following swift and summary courts martial, the executions began. Plunkett was scheduled to be shot at dawn on 4th May. He and Grace married late on the evening before, in Kilmainham Jail. She saw him for the last time in his cell, shortly before he was shot. As the facts unfolded and were reported in newspapers, at home and abroad, the impact on public opinion was enormous. The story of the prison wedding, which has been compared to something akin to the novels of Honoré de Balzac, touched the hearts of people in a unique way. Overnight, Grace became a tragic heroine. Her fate was immediately linked to that of Sarah Curran, the beloved of Robert Emmet, who had been executed following a previous attempt to free Ireland, by armed insurrection, in 1803.

Grace and Joseph Mary Plunkett were both twenty-eight years old at the time of their marriage. There was nothing apparent in Grace's background that made such a fate likely, or prepared her for the consequences. Her love-affair, and eventual engagement, met with opposition from her parents and some of those in her social circle were astonished by her choice of husband. Those who knew her best, however, were not surprised. Their support and friendship were to be of crucial importance to her in the years that followed.

Grace's background differed from that of her husband, though there were some cultural similarities. She was born on 4th March, 1888 in

1

ÉIRE   IRELAND

Acht um Chlarú Pósadh, 1863. Foirm A.

Registration of Marriages Act, 1863. Form A.

Pósadh a Solátanaíodh i
Marriage Solemnised at the Catholic _Chapel_ of _Kilmainham Prison_

i gContae
in the Registrar's District of _Mid Kilmainham_

i gContae Chláraitheora Maoirseachta,
in the Superintendent Registrar's District of _South Dublin_

i gContae
in the County of _City of Dublin_

Uimh. No. 1	Dáta um Pósadh When Married 2	Ainm agus Sloinne Name and Surname 3	Aois Age 4	Riail Condition 5	Céim nó Slí Bheatha Rank or Profession 6	Ionad Cónaithe Residence at the time of Marriage 7	Ainm agus Sloinne an Athar Father's Name and Surname 8	Céim Bheatha nó Athar Rank or Profession of Father 9
214	3rd May 1916	Joseph Plunkett	Full	Bachelor	Gentleman	Kilmainham Prison &c.	Count George Noble Plunkett	Director Dublin Museum
		Grace Gifford	Full	Spinster	Artist	29 Oakley Road Rathmines	Frederick Gifford	Solicitor

Arna bPósadh i
Married in the Catholic _Chapel_ of _Kilmainham Prison_ de réir Uird agus Gnáthaí na hEaglaise Caitlicighe,
according to the Rites and Ceremonies of the Catholic Church by me.

Síníthe _Eugene McCarthy_

Solátanaíodh an Pósadh
so Eadrainne
This Marriage was
Solemnised between us,
{ Joseph Plunkett
  Grace Gifford }

In ár bhFianaise
In the Presence of us
{ Eugene McCarthy
  John Lackey Byrd &c. Royal Dublin Fusiliers }

In fhef céilp i seo de thaifid atá i gClár-leabhair na bPósadh i n-Oifig an Ard-Chláraitheora i mbaile Atha Cliath.
Certified to be a true copy taken from the Certified Copies of Entries of Marriages in Oifig an Ard-Chláraitheora, Dublin.

Tugtha fá Shéala Oifige an Ard-Chláraitheora
Given under the Seal of Oifig an Ard-Chláraitheora

an} _Nineteenth_
this}   14 to to
            day of } _September_ 19 90

Ath-Scríofa _ADG_   Scrúdaithe _DHS_
Copied   Examined

Is cion trom é an tuarisc seo a mhrú nó á cháil tairlú a athraíthe.

TO ALTER THIS DOCUMENT OR TO UTTER IT SO ALTERED IS A SERIOUS OFFENCE

2

Grace
Gifford

Joseph
Plunkett

the comfortable family home of her parents at 8, Temple Villas in Rathmines, a handsome and leafy inner suburb of Dublin city. Her father, Frederick Gifford, was a prosperous solicitor. His wife Isabella, née Burton, shared his strong Unionist political views. They were of different religions, Frederick being a Roman Catholic while Isabella was a Protestant. They had a family of twelve children, of whom Grace was the second youngest. In accordance with the custom of the time for 'mixed marriages', the daughters were raised in the Protestant faith, while the sons followed their father's Catholicism. This custom, known as the 'Palatine Pact' seems on the whole to have worked in a harmonious way, creating less resentment than the later system imposed by the Catholic Church in the 'Ne Temere' decree in 1908.[1] That measure insisted that all children of mixed marriages must be raised as Catholics, and the Protestant partner had to promise this before the marriage could take place. (This system has been relaxed in recent times to allow more flexibility in a mixed faith union.)

The Gifford children were lively, articulate and affectionate amongst themselves. They had all the comforts of a prosperous home, a wide circle of friends and good educational opportunities. Some sources, however, state that the home was not a happy one. Isabella Gifford was not fond of children but the conventions and mores of the period forced her into frequent pregnancies. She was a strong Protestant who attempted to force the same rigid views on her daughters. The Unionist political views of both parents were to be challenged as the girls grew up. Grace later said that the influence of their Catholic and nationalist nurse-maids had a big impact on herself and her sisters. The boys developed into either half-hearted Unionists or Fabian Socialists, while four of the sisters became strong rebels who supported the struggle for Irish freedom.

No information survives about where the Gifford sisters received their early education. It is probable that they were sent to one of the many private schools in the locality. Later, Grace and her sister Sydney, went to Alexandra School, then in the centre of Dublin.[2]

The entire background and upbringing of the family was later castigated by Sydney, the youngest child, who became a writer and propagandist for Ireland's claim to independence.[3] Sydney was born on 3rd August, 1889. She saw Rathmines as a stronghold of British Imperialism, the residents 'inanimate models' of English people. Sydney found the atmosphere stifling – one in which any new thought, or independence of action, was automatically seen as 'eccentric'. She disliked the neighbours who lived close to her, with their 'strange, synthetic English accents, their snobbery and their half-hearted desire to be a ruling caste'.[4] Likewise, she was critical of Alexandra School, seeing it as a snobbish, West British establishment which ignored Irish history and culture and trained its pupils to look down on the ordinary people of Ireland as inferior 'natives'.

Later in her life, Grace also spoke critically of the standards of education at Alexandra. But, at the time, she was intent on studying at the Dublin Metropolitan School of Art, where she eventually became a pupil in 1904 when she was sixteen. There was a strong vein of artistic talent in the Gifford family. Isabella's uncle, Frederick William Burton, had been a distinguished artist in the nineteenth century. Born in Corofin, County Clare in 1816, he excelled as a watercolourist. He travelled about Ireland with his friend George Petrie, a fellow painter and antiquarian. Both were deeply interested in Irish history, folklore and legends. Burton was a painstaking artist who made careful preliminary sketches in pen or pencil before taking up his colours and brushes. Connemara and the West of Ireland generally had a particular fascination for him. Perhaps his best known picture in Ireland, now in the National Gallery, is that of the Aran fisherman with his drowned child. However, his greatest painting is generally considered to be that of the doomed lovers, Hellilil and Hildebrand. Their story, taken from a Danish ballad, was one Burton had learned about while living in Bavaria. At that time he was working for King Maximilian II as an adviser on the Royal collection.

Before Grace attended the School of Art, her brother Gabriel Paul and her sister Ada had studied there. (Both of them subsequently left Ireland for the United States of America.) The Dublin Metropolitan School of Art had been established in 1877. It followed the School that the Royal Dublin Society had organised, taking pupils from the middle of the eighteenth century onwards. In Grace's time, the school was greatly influenced by the Department of Agriculture and Technical Instruction, which operated from 1900. The main emphasis was on teaching technology and design. Another institution, the Royal Hibernian Academy, taught art in other areas. This led to a number of anomalies in the system. When Grace began her studies, the school had approximately 500 pupils of whom about 300 attended day classes while the remainder went to the evening sessions. There were no tests for admission so people of all ages and abilities could enrol. Grace was a day student travelling in and out of the city by either electric trams, or by bicycle. Cycling then was extremely popular, regarded as healthy exercise as well as a means of transport.

All classes in the school were taught drawing from the antique and from life, objects and plants. They were also taught to design patterns for the lace industry. Instruction was given on stained glass and enamel work. This emphasis on utility caused some frustrations among both the students and their teachers. An earlier pupil at the school was the future poet William Butler Yeats. He wrote later that he found the system boring and destructive of all kinds of individuality and enthusiasm. Consequently, Yeats gave up art and decided to make literature his future career.

Among Grace's teachers was the very successful William Orpen, who is said to have regarded her as one of his most talented pupils. Orpen was born in Dublin in 1878. His father, like Grace's, was a successful solicitor. His talent for art was seen from a very early age and he went to the Dublin School of Art when he was twelve, in 1891. He later studied at the Slade School in London where he enjoyed meteoric success. Orpen became a close friend of Augustus John and got to know his fellow students who later formed part of the London artistic establishment. Orpen's strong personality proved somewhat overpowering to some of his pupils, but Grace was never intimidated by him. Orpen admired both Grace's talent and her strong humourous personality. He often sketched her portrait in her student days and eventually painted her as one of his subjects for a series on 'Young Ireland'.

The School of Art was a very pro-establishment institution and most of the teachers and students came from Unionist families who were also Protestant. The nominal head of the Department of Agriculture and Technical Instruction was the Chief Secretary, but the real political head from 1900–1907 was Horace Plunkett who had worked hard to have it established. Plunkett was a son of Lord Dunsany and belonged to the Protestant branch of the family. Lord Dunsany was an extensive landowner, and Horace became a pioneer of agricultural co-operation as first president of the Irish Agricultural Organisation Society founded in 1894. For a time he was a Member of Parliament for South County Dublin and a member of the Congested Districts' Board which was set up in 1891 to help the poorest parts of Ireland. Plunkett was a hard-working patriot who supported Unionist politics because he believed the country was not fit for independence.

Grace's talent for caricature was soon discovered and developed. She was one of an emerging group of women artists taught by Orpen. They included Beatrice Elvery, Estella Solomons, Margaret Crilly and Kathleen Fox. Despite her criticisms of the teachers and the system, Grace enjoyed her time as a student. She often attended evening classes where she met a different group of students including William (known as Willie) Pearse, the brother of Patrick. He was there to train as a sculptor for work in his father's stone-carving business, then situated in Great Brunswick Street. Willie dressed in an artistic way, with flowing dark hair, a floppy tie and sometimes wore a kilt. He introduced classes in Irish to the students and was one of a small band of nationalists attending the school.

Grace also came into the school for social functions such as dances. These were lively occasions where the students could relax and mix together. A highlight was the Nine Arts Ball, a fancy dress affair which took place every year in the Metropole Hotel.

Both staff and students were involved in many projects reflecting the Celtic Revival. These included the decoration of Loughrea Cathedral and the Honan Chapel in Cork. Bronze statues of Irish heroes by Oliver Sheppard and the stained glass of Harry Clarke and Michael Healy were specially remarkable in the first two decades of the century.

Grace won two prizes in her first two years as a student – one for 'Drawing on the Blackboard and Freehand Drawing' and the second for 'Drawing on the Blackboard and Model Drawing'.[5] In accordance with custom, the prizes were presented by the Viceroy. Lord Aberdeen did the honours on 27th February, 1906, and his wife the following year on 30th January, 1907. Lady Aberdeen was a staunch supporter of the School of Art. She had a particular interest in the revival of crafts and had founded the Irish Association in 1886 to market products such as Irish lace. During her husband's second term as Viceroy, she invited the art students to design embroidery for the costume she was to wear at the Coronation of King Edward VII in 1902. In 1909, she invited the students to supply costume designs for the Irish Industries Project she organised that year.

Dublin was a vibrant city in Grace's youth. The cultural renaissance of the Celtic Revival was in full flow. All sorts of activities from the Gaelic League to new departures in literature, drama, music and the arts were flourishing. Hugh Lane became the driving force in art. Born in County Cork in 1875, Lane spent much of his youth travelling on the continent with his mother. He set up as a picture dealer in London at an early age. His great flair and talent soon made him a wealthy man and he was knighted in 1909. After meeting W. B. Yeats at the home of his aunt, Lady Gregory, his interest in Irish art developed. His great energy and enthusiasm drew many supporters who worked hard to found a Gallery of Modern Art in Dublin. Grace was almost certainly a visitor to the Staats Forbes exhibition of modern art at the Royal Hibernian Academy in 1904. This made a great impression in Dublin.

Grace was out of Dublin for the year 1907–1908. She continued her studies at the Slade School of Art in London, where she followed a full-time course in Fine Art. She lived close to the school at 113, Gower Street. When she returned to Dublin, she began the difficult task of trying to earn her living as a caricaturist. She was anxious to become independent as soon as possible. At one time she became so despondent about her prospects that she considered emigration. However, she was reluctant to take that course and decided against it in the end.

Meanwhile Grace's sisters had begun their own journeys into adult life. Muriel became a student nurse at Sir Patrick Dun's hospital in Dublin. Katie, the eldest girl, studied languages and later graduated from the Royal University, which preceded the present University College in Dublin. Nellie became a teacher of domestic economy in County Meath. This occupation taught her a lot about country life, hitherto almost unknown territory to the very urban Gifford family. Nellie stayed in labourers' cottages and saw rural poverty and land hunger at close quarters. Sydney's path to a career as a writer began when she started to read Arthur Griffith's Sinn Féin newspaper, which promoted his ideas of self-reliance in politics and economics. Sydney began to send articles to Griffith and was delighted when they were published. Like other writers who admired and wrote for Griffith, she did not expect or receive payment. She learned her craft in this way, and later became a skilled writer, using the name John Brennan as her pseudonym. Sydney and her sisters first met Griffith when they were invited by the poet Seamus O'Sullivan to visit him at the Martello

Tower in Sandycove on the south coast of County Dublin.[6] Griffith rowed the girls around Dublin Bay that summer afternoon. Sydney was impressed by his relaxed behaviour in private which was in contrast to his rather stern public persona.[7]

The Gifford sisters were attractive, lively and stylishly dressed. It was said that the gloomy Sinn Féin office at 6, Harcourt Street in Dublin took on the appearance of a 'flower garden' when they were there. Obviously good social mixers, they went about so much that if one of them spent an evening at home, their father Frederick would enquire with heavy sarcasm 'What is the matter? I hope you are not ill?'[8]

It was an Irish woman journalist working in London – Mrs Dryhurst – who began to lead the girls into new social circles. One of their brothers, then working in London, met Mrs Dryhurst and showed her some of Sydney's articles. Shortly afterwards, on a visit to Dublin, she met the Gifford family and became a strong influence on the daughters. She brought them to visit George Russell, the poet and painter known as Æ who worked in the Co-operative movement. He and his wife were 'At Home' to all their friends on Sunday evenings in Rathgar. Their wide circle included writers and artists such as John Butler Yeats with his sons Willie and Jack, Padraic Colum, James Stephens and many others. Constance Markievicz was often there with her Polish husband, as were Sarah Purser and the incredibly beautiful Maud Gonne. For this visit Mrs Dryhurst had dressed her protégées in colourful, foreign costumes, of which she had a collection. On arrival in Rathgar, the sisters were surprised to find the other guests in ordinary clothes. Bashfully they removed themselves to the smaller of the two reception rooms, then empty of other guests![9]

The opening of St Enda's School on Oakley Road, Ranelagh,[10] was to bring the Gifford girls into direct contact with the future leaders of 1916. The school was for boys. It aimed at a fully Irish education whereby the pupils would study the language and culture of their own country and take part in activities such as drama, sport and music. The school was bilingual and its emphasis was on training the boys to take their part in a free and Gaelic Ireland which was the aspiration of the founder Patrick Pearse and his assistant Thomas MacDonagh. Mrs Dryhurst was very interested in what she had heard of this new type of education. In her commanding way, she brought Sydney and her sisters to see the school and its teachers shortly after it opened in 1908.

9

It was Thomas MacDonagh who came bounding down the steps to greet them. Mrs Dryhurst introduced the girls by their first names and then advised him that he should 'fall in love with one of these girls and marry her'! This blatant attempt at match-making could have paralysed the young people, but MacDonagh's quick wit came to the rescue. He laughed and said: 'That would be easy – the only difficulty would be to decide which one![11] The rest of the visit was on a more serious note. Sydney later described her first impressions of Pearse and MacDonagh. Pearse was a little above medium height, broadly built with dark hair, grey eyes and a pale complexion. His expression and conversation were rather solemn, but he spoke easily. MacDonagh was different in both appearance and personality. He was small but sturdily built, with curly brown hair and large grey eyes. He had a strong Tipperary accent, a lively manner and a mischievous sense of humour. His conversation impressed Sydney with its great wit and sparkle. All the sisters found the visit an unusual experience which left them with plenty to think about afterwards.

Grace did not meet her future husband until some years later. Meanwhile, her interests, apart from art, were expanding in various directions. As she went about Dublin she became aware of the grinding poverty and hardship in the back streets of the city. Close to the handsome Georgian Squares and the many fine public buildings lay a squalor and misery that she saw for the first time. Much of this poverty was due to the large number of unskilled workers who could only get casual and badly-paid employment. Their health was poor, their living conditions substandard. Even at the best of times, they seemed doomed to live on the edge of destitution. Grace's social conscience was stirred and she began to look for ways to help this pathetic underclass.

In 1908, Mrs Dryhurst brought Sydney to a meeting of the Daughters of Erin (in Irish, Inghinidhe na h-Eireann), the revolutionary women's group founded by Maud Gonne eight years earlier. The group worked hard for the complete independence of Ireland. Much of its work was educational. Classes were organised in Irish history, language, drama and elocution. The drama classes trained several girls who later became successful on the stage – Molly and Sara Allgood, Mary Walker (known as Maire Ni Shiubhlaigh) and Maire Quinn who later married the actor Dudley Digges. Jennie Wyse Power, the patriot and feminist, and Sinéad Flanagan, who later married Eamon de Valera were also active in the group. Vigorous propaganda work was done by the women, particularly in opposing British imperialism and the recruiting of Irish boys and men into the British Army.

The meeting that Sydney attended also saw the first appearance there of Constance Markievicz. It was an evening meeting and Constance came late, attired in full evening dress following a social function. Most of the women present were plainly dressed in costumes of Donegal tweed. They viewed with suspicion this tall, beautiful woman who burst upon them. But, as the meeting went on, Constance's obvious sincerity changed their attitude to her. The Daughters were planning to launch a new paper to be called 'Bean na h-Eireann' (Woman of Ireland). Constance joined in the lively discussion of this project and by the end of the evening she was accepted as a member of the group. She later wrote the gardening notes for the paper, using the pen-names of 'Armid' and 'Macha'.

In 1910, James Connolly, the Labour leader, asked Maud Gonne and her helpers to support his scheme to supply school meals for the poor children of the inner city. As this had been one of Maud Gonne's own cherished plans, she readily agreed. The first meals were supplied in the Catholic parish of St Audoen and later extended to other areas. We find Grace's name among the helpers with those of two of her sisters, Muriel and Sydney.

The movement to obtain votes for women also found staunch supporters in the Gifford sisters. The constitutional campaign began in Dublin in 1876, founded by a courageous couple, Anna Haslam and her husband Thomas. Both were members of the religious group known as the Quakers, more formally the Society of Friends. Despite hard and persistent work, its peaceful methods failed to gain widespread support for the cause. A more militant group, the 'Irish Women's Franchise League' was started in Dublin in 1908 by Hanna Sheehy Skeffington and Margaret Cousins. This new body was more aggressive in its tactics. There was a strong presence of young women who, like Hanna Sheehy Skeffington, had obtained university degrees. The majority were nationalists in contrast to the older group, most of whose members were unionists. Men were allowed to be associate members. Hanna's husband Frank was a strong campaigner and later edited the excellent paper, the *Irish Citizen*, which promoted the cause. The two suffrage societies worked in tandem and relations were cordial despite the different methods adopted by the younger women. Grace, together with her sisters Nellie, Muriel and Sydney, became a strong supporter of the new League.[12]

We catch another glimpse of Grace's activities in the year 1911. She joined a group of women, led by Maud Gonne, who protested outside City Hall against a proposed 'Loyal Address' from Dublin Corporation to King George V and his consort Queen Mary. The royal couple were due to visit Ireland in accordance with custom. A new monarch made visits throughout Britain and overseas with the aim of meeting people and being welcomed by them. On the death of Queen Victoria in 1901, the visit of her son Edward VII was met by widespread nationalist protest. Nevertheless, on that occasion Dublin Corporation had voted for the Loyal Address to the new king. In 1911, stronger efforts were made to stop such a demonstration of loyalty to unionism, and in the end, the members of Dublin Corporation defeated the proposal.

The year 1912 brought a dramatic change in Irish politics. Due to the removal of the veto of the House of Lords the year before, Home Rule for Ireland became a real possibility. As a result, the reputation of John Redmond and his Parliamentary Party began to rise in public opinion. Most people hoped that constitutional politics would at last achieve a measure of independence for Ireland. However, several barriers threatened to block the way, notably the gathering storm clouds in the north where the loyalists had found a new leader in Edward Carson. There was also the fact that Arthur Griffith and other leaders of nationalist opinion considered the proposed Bill inadequate and said so publicly. Griffith was angered by the proposed financial provisions and by a clause that allowed the British parliament to amend laws passed by the Irish assembly. The issue of votes for women also came to a head in 1912 when Redmond clashed with those who demanded that votes for women be included in the Home Rule Bill.

Grace became a frequent visitor to the United Arts Club in this period. The Club had been founded in 1907 by Count Casimir Markievicz, his wife Constance and Ellen Duncan. Its premises were at 44, St Stephen's Green in the centre of the city. The varied circle of the Club included William Butler Yeats, his brother Jack, Frank Cruise O'Brien, Thomas Bodkin, Dermod O'Brien, Lennox Robinson and Katherine Tynan Hinkson. The political views of the members varied but most of them were unionists who opposed the Home Rule Bill. The company in the Club has been described as 'not bookish or intellectual' and Grace, who first appears in the records as the guest of Count Markievicz in 1912, would have enjoyed the lively, Bohemian atmosphere.[13]

The 1913 general strike or lock-out of Dublin workers revealed deep divisions in the Club. The lock-out was an attempt by William Martin Murphy and other employers to break the power of the Irish Transport and General Workers' Union, which was founded and led by James Larkin in 1909. The support of Constance Markievicz for Larkin and James Connolly led many in the Club and elsewhere to regard her as a traitor to her class. The Countess worked hard to feed the starving workers and their families during the lock-out. Police violence in August that year led to many protests, including one by Count Markievicz who wrote to the Under-Secretary at Dublin Castle.[14]

Meanwhile, Grace was still struggling to establish her career as an artist. Her early cartoons of well-known people were beginning to be admired. Thus we find Major John MacBride, future participant in the 1916 rising, writing to thank Grace for a sketch she had sent him and informing her of his intention to have it framed and keep it with his 'war relics'.[15] Her other early subjects included George Russell (Æ) depicted as a 'grizzly bear', Professor John Pentland Mahaffy of Trinity College, Dublin on a design for a Greek vase, and Doctor George Sigerson, the distinguished Celtic scholar and writer who was portrayed as 'Saint George Slaying Dragons'. Despite her growing reputation, earning a full living was still difficult for Grace. Her older brother Gabriel Paul had emigrated to the United States of America where he continued his career as an artist. But Grace loved Dublin and decided to stay there. In accordance with the general custom of the time for unmarried girls, she still lived in the home of her parents. This did not restrict her too much and she found ways to take part in activities of which her parents – especially her mother Isabella – would not have approved. As time passed, the conventional outlook of her parents and their circle became more irksome to her.

George Russell (Æ) poet and painter. He worked for the Irish Agricultural Organisation Society to promote co-operation in farming. The D.A.T.I. was the Department of Agriculture and Technical Instruction.

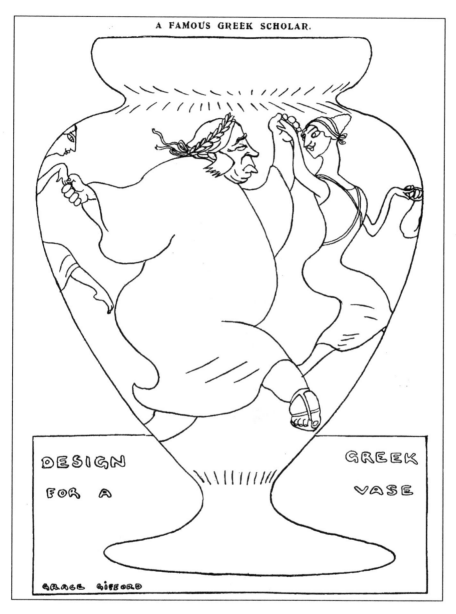

Professor John Pentland Mahaffy who taught Ancient History in Trinity
College, Dublin and became Provost of that College.

Dr. George Sigerson, physician and man of letters. His best-known work 'Bards of the Gael and Gall' appeared in 1897 and consisted of a collection of poetry which he translated from Irish. His home at 3 Clare Street Dublin was a centre of hospitality for those who shared his interests in Irish literature and music.

NOTES

1. See *New Catholic Encyclopaedia*, Vol.10.
2. The records of the school only show the name of Sydney. It may be that Grace was only there for a very short time.
3. Sydney Gifford Czira *The Years Flew By* (Gifford and Craven, 1974). Her pen-name was John Brennan.
4. *Ibid.*, pp.6–7.
5. The lists of prizewinners are given in the Headmasters' reports. A full history of the teaching of art in Dublin is given in: Professor John Turpin *A School of Art in Dublin since the Eighteeenth Century* (Gill and Macmillan, 1995).
6. The tower now houses the James Joyce Museum.
7. Sydney Gifford Czira, *op. cit.*, pp.32–33.
8. *Ibid.*, p.33.
9. *Ibid.*, pp.11–12.
10. Ranelagh is an inner suburb of Dublin.
11. Sydney Gifford Czira, *op. cit.*, p.18.
12. A full account of the IWFL is given in: James and Margaret Cousins *We Two Together*, published in Madras, India in 1950. See also Margaret Ward *Hanna Sheehy Skeffington* (Attic Press, 1997).
13. See Patricia Boylan *All Cultivated People: A History of the United Arts Club, Dublin* (Colin Smythe, 1988), p.32.
14. *Ibid.*, p.72.
15. The original letter dated 17 July 1912 is in the custody of Ann Burke. The War relics were those of the Boer War when MacBride fought against the British.

CHAPTER TWO

Joseph Mary Plunkett

JOSEPH MARY PLUNKETT was slightly older than his future wife. He was born on 21st November, 1887 at 26, Upper Fitzwilliam Street in the centre of Dublin. He belonged to the Catholic branch of a distinguished family who had played a part in Irish history for about six hundred years. Many of them had landed estates, notably the Earls of Fingall and Dunsany in County Meath. They cherished the memory of their kinsman, Archbishop Oliver Plunkett, now venerated as a saint by the Roman Catholic Church.[1] He had been martyred at Tyburn in London in 1681 following trumped-up charges of involvement in the Titus Oates conspiracy. That so-called 'Popish Plot' had caused widespread panic in England and it increased the persecution of Catholics which was then the government policy in both England and Ireland.

Joseph Mary's paternal grandfather Patrick had left the family farm in County Meath at the time of the great famine that followed the failure of the potato crop. He came to Dublin to seek a living in either 1846 or 1847. Patrick married Elizabeth Murphy, a widow who had a leather shop in Aungier Street. Her father, John Noble, of Italian or half-Italian origin, had a leather shop on the opposite side of Aungier Street. Elizabeth's mother, an O'Sullivan from Tralee, is reputed to have known Ann Devlin, the faithful servant of Robert Emmet and visited her when she was dying.[2]

After Patrick's marriage, the business was carried on in his name. He prospered and started to build houses in the Rathmines area of Dublin, where he lived at 3, Belgrave Road. He eventually settled all this property on his son, George Noble, who was the only surviving child of his first marriage. Elizabeth died when George was twenty-one. Patrick then married Helena O'Sullivan, a cousin of Elizabeth, with whom he had a second family of four children.

Tuberculosis ran in the Plunkett family and for this reason George, who was born in Aungier Street in 1851, was brought to Europe for a time. He became a pupil at a boarding school in Nice, then part of Italy. Later, in 1866 and 1867, he attended the Jesuit school at Clongowes Wood in County Kildare. He went on to study law at Trinity College and became a barrister. While he was there, he offered a medal for Gaelic which was won by Douglas Hyde. Though it has been said that George was not good in Court,[3] law and politics occupied him until the death of Parnell in 1891. George had greatly admired the political genius of that 'lost leader' whose predecessor, Isaac Butt, he had also known. Redmond, the later leader of the Irish Parliamentary Party, refused to sponsor Plunkett as a candidate. They differed on the Liberal policy of free trade. Redmond supported it but Plunkett favoured a system of tariffs to help the Irish economy. Having been thus frustrated in his wish for a political career, George turned to art and literature. He wrote articles for nationalist and cultural papers and some art criticism. He lectured to many cultural bodies. For a time he was secretary of the Society for the Preservation of the Irish Language which preceded the Gaelic League. He also wrote poetry and collected Irish music. A devout Catholic, he received the honour of becoming a Papal Count in recognition of his services to the Church. This was a hereditary title conferred in or about the year 1884.

George had married in 1883. His bride was Josephine Cranny, the daughter of a successful businessman who had become a builder and developer of property. Patrick Cranny came from Borris in County Carlow. He settled in Dublin, where his first business venture was a shoe shop in South Great Georges Street. It prospered and he later sold it. He built houses in Ballsbridge, Donnybrook and Rathmines, all inner suburbs of the city. He also built Muckross Park on Marlborough Road in Donnybrook as a home for himself and his family.[4] When Josephine married George Plunkett, the wedding reception was held in that impressive setting. The bride received a generous dowry of nearby houses from her father. The young couple went to the United States of America for their honeymoon. They extended the visit to spend some time searching for a missing relative. On their return to Dublin, they settled in Fitzwilliam Street. The couple had seven children: Philomena (known as 'Mimi'), Joseph Mary, Moya, Geraldine, George, Josephine (known as 'Fiona') and John.

Joseph Mary, known as 'Joe' to his family, was a delicate child. His first school was the Catholic University primary school in Lower Leeson Street close to his home. Before the year 1900, Joe had suffered both pneumonia and pleurisy. His mother brought him to France to spend the winter in the warmer climate there. Her plans changed when she herself became ill in Paris. She left her son at a Marist boarding school in Passy. Family recollection has not been kind to Joe's mother. She was not a domesticated woman and allowed her children to run wild without taking care of their health or superivising their activities in the normal way.[5] She is said to have left Joe in Paris without warm clothes to withstand the winter weather there. When he came back to Dublin he had tubercular glands in his neck. Later these were removed in the crude way of the time, leaving heavy scars.

His father later wrote that Joe was a lively boy despite poor health. He read deeply as he grew up. His secondary education, after his return from Paris, was at Belvedere College, the Jesuit school on the north side of Dublin. As a day pupil he had to cross the city from Kilternan Abbey, where the family was then living. This was about eight miles outside the city on the south side. Geraldine Plunkett believed these tiring journeys were detrimental to Joe's health.[6] Joe was an avid student with a particular interest in Catholic philosophy. He perused the writings of Saint Thomas Aquinas and other mystics. The poetry of St John of the Cross influenced him deeply and increased, what have been called, his 'sacrificial tendencies'.[7] Joe was subsequently sent to the English Jesuit School at Stonyhurst in Lancashire. There he acquired some military training and knowledge from the Officers' Training Corps in the school. Summer manoeuvres on Salisbury Plain gave him experience which he was later to use in making plans for an Irish insurrection. Joe spent two years at Stonyhurst, where he made a particular study of philosophy. When he returned to Dublin he was twenty years of age. The family home to which he returned was a place of 'hair-splitting argument', according to Joe's sister Geraldine, and this increased with his presence there. Obviously the young adults were a lively lot.

Count Plunkett had been appointed as Director of the National Museum of Science and Art in 1907. Deeply involved as he was in the cultural life of his native city, the Count must have been a strong influence on his children. He often lectured abroad on art, a task that came easily to him as he was a splendid linguist, particularly in French and Italian. He continued to have a deep interest in politics and watched closely the parliamentary struggle to obtain Home Rule for Ireland. His own views became more radical and republican as time passed.

Meanwhile, Joe's poor health led to his spending long periods abroad, particularly in the winter months. He went to Italy, France, Sicily and Malta, and during these stays, became fluent in several languages. He also learned some Arabic during a later visit to Algeria. As he grew to maturity he developed many talents. Ultimately he was best known for his poetry though he could also draw and paint, play both piano and violin and was a talented actor. He loved all physical exercise, particularly roller-skating and dancing. He continued to be a fervent Catholic with a mystical streak which was shown in his poetry.

When he was back in Dublin in 1910, Joe began to study the Irish language with a view to passing the matriculation examination of the National University. His mother had heard about St Enda's school and believed Thomas MacDonagh would be a suitable teacher for her son. She brought Joe to the school to discuss the matter. This introduction had an immediate impact on both young men. MacDonagh, who at the age of thirty-two was nine years older than his pupil, was instantly charmed by the younger boy with his wide learning and witty tongue. The lessons in Irish proceeded rapidly and successfully and the two became close personal friends. They had many ideals, tastes and personal qualities in common. Both were scholars by nature, wrote poetry and were devoted to the arts, especially theatre and literature. MacDonagh was less religious by temperament but kept to the Catholic faith in which he had been reared. Both young men were ardent patriots. They believed Irish independence would only be achieved by an armed struggle in their generation. Plans for this would have to be made in the immediate future.[8]

However, their first joint ventures were in the cultural sphere. The 'Theatre of Ireland' occupied them on a regular basis. This was a valiant effort, to produce new plays by Irish dramatists with very little money. The performances were held in a hall in Hardwicke Street, a premises owned and lent to the performers by Joe's mother. The group managed to produce a season of new plays from 1906 to 1915. Many rehearsals took place in the 'ice-cold basement' of the Sinn Féin headquarters at 6, Harcourt Street. Among the plays produced were *The Land* by

Padraic Colum, *Deirdre* by George Russell (Æ) and *The Turn of the Road* by Rutherford Mayne. Other playwrights who contributed to the productions included Jane Barlow, James Stephens and Edward Martyn. Thomas MacDonagh wrote two plays for the group, the second of which, *The Pagan*, was the last production before the theatre closed.

Thomas MacDonagh and Professor Davy Houston started a new literary magazine, *The Irish Review*, in 1911. It included articles on current affairs and social questions in which new ideas were expressed. An article by Roger Casement in 1913 caused some discussion on Irish political thinking. It was entitled 'Ireland, Germany and the Freedom of the Sea' and expressed Casement's view that England's maritime supremacy had had disastrous results for Europe and the wider world. This dominance of the seas depended, to some extent, on British occupation of Ireland. By this time, Joe Plunkett had taken over the magazine. He raised money to pay off debts and increased the amount of space given to more controversial subjects. A second article by Casement supported the idea of a volunteer force to defend Ireland's neutrality if war broke out in Europe.

In 1911, while Joe Plunkett was spending the winter months in Algeria, his first book of poetry, *The Circle and the Sword*, was published. Thomas MacDonagh saw it through the press and the book was dedicated to him. By this time, Plunkett was recognised as a significant poet of his generation. He was first and foremost a mystical one, with what has been described as 'an unique and visionary intensity'.[9] Of course, his verse had faults of vagueness and obscurity. It must be assumed that, had he lived longer, his talent would have developed more fully. Nevertheless, what he left behind is impressive as a legacy of his ability, outlook and aspirations. At a time when many young men felt they had a rendezvous with death, Plunkett, like Pearse, foretold his own fate:[10]

> Rougher than death the road I choose
> Yet shall my feet not walk astray,
> Though dark, my way I shall not lose
> For this way is the darkest way.

He wrote explicitly of blood sacrifice:

> Praise God if this my blood fulfils the doom
> When you, dark Rose, shall redden into bloom.

The Circle and the Sword collection included what has become Plunkett's best-known poem, 'I see His blood upon the Rose', which expresses his deep Catholic faith and devotion.

From 1913 onwards, all Joe's activities were directed towards planning an armed insurrection to free Ireland. The general strike or lockout in Dublin that year became a catalyst for social and political change. Many people, even those of conservative opinions, were upset by the events of that crisis which lasted for four months. Joe's future sister-in-law, Nellie Gifford, by then a strong Labour supporter, was deeply involved in events. Centres had been set up to feed the starving workers and their families, notably Constance Markievicz's Liberty Hall canteen. The Countess also sheltered many of the strikers in her home at Surrey House in Rathmines and James Larkin stayed there when he was forced to go 'on the run'. When Larkin was there the police watched the house. To throw them off the scent, a party was organised. Most of the guests were artistic and theatrical friends of the Count and his wife who had no connection with politics. The windows of the house were opened wide and lights were lit in all the rooms. This ruse succeeded and the guard of police in plain clothes was withdrawn.

On 31st August of that year, while staying at the Countess's house, Larkin was due to speak at the Imperial Hotel. The problem of getting him there had to be resolved. It was decided to disguise him as an elderly clergyman and, to avoid recognition of his voice with its strong Liverpool accent, a 'niece' was to accompany him and do all the talking. The role fell to Nellie Gifford. Both the Count and Larkin were very tall men. Larkin was dressed in his host's top hat and frockcoat. Helena Molony disguised him by powdering grey his black hair and attaching a grey beard to his chin. A pair of glasses were added to shorten the appearance of Larkin's long nose.

A cab was called to the house for the 'Reverend Mr Donnelly' and his niece. In due time it reached the hotel. Larkin threw off his disguise before speaking to the crowd from one of the hotel balconies. He was quickly arrested by police who were watching the scene. The crowd outside was dispersed by a baton charge so brutal that the day became known as 'Bloody Sunday', one of the many occasions in Irish history to be so described. A direct result was the founding of the Irish Citizen Army to protect the workers in future. James Connolly organised it from Liberty Hall, the headquarters of the Irish Transport and General Workers' Union. Nellie Gifford became a member.

When the 1913 lock-out came to an end, the workers were defeated, but they had gained a certain moral victory. Many people saw the industrial dispute as sowing some of the seeds for the 1916 Rising. Joe Plunkett was one of many whose political views hardened in those months. As he saw it, real social change could only come to Ireland when full political independence was achieved. When he saw the newspaper notice of a public meeting to form the Volunteers in November, he went to see Eoin MacNeill, the distinguished Gaelic scholar who had been one of the founders of the Gaelic League. MacNeill had suggested the formation of the Volunteers and Joe went to offer his services. He already knew MacNeill quite well and told him that while his health might not allow him to be 'much of a soldier' he was prepared to use the *Irish Review* as propaganda for the Volunteers. Subsequently, Joe attended a public meeting in the Rotunda where the new group was founded. Between three and four thousand enthusiastic recruits joined at once. Joe was elected to the executive. By May 1914, the number of Volunteers had risen to about seventy-five thousand. Following the example of the Ulster Volunteers, arms were obtained in July and August by successful gun-running at Howth in Dublin and Kilcoole in Wicklow. The outbreak of the European war on 4th August opened a new phase in the history of the Volunteers. John Redmond, the leader of the Irish Parliamentary Party at Westminster, had at last succeeded in having a Home Rule Act for Ireland passed into law. Earlier, worried by what he saw as a private army, he had been given some superficial control of the Volunteers through nomination of members to the Provisional Committee, which governed their organisation. At first, Redmond intended that the Volunteers would be used to defend Home Rule against threats from Ulster, but, on the outbreak of war, he pledged Ireland's support for the war effort and stated that defence of the island against any foreign foe could be left to Irishmen – to the Volunteers in both parts of the country. Speaking at Woodenbridge in Wicklow on 20th September, Redmond went further. He urged the Volunteers not just to defend Ireland but to go 'wherever the firing-line extends'. As the operation of the Home Rule Act had been suspended for the duration of the war, many people thought this call was excessive. It caused an immediate split in the Volunteers. The majority followed Redmond's call and many young men enlisted in the British forces. A minority of about eleven thousand remained and kept the title of 'Irish Volunteers'. The separatist core of those who remained in Ireland was determined to make a strike for freedom while Britain was occupied elsewhere.

Whilst many movements contributed to the 1916 Rising, in its final stages it was planned by the Irish Republican Brotherhood, the oath-bound secret society that had infiltrated the Irish Volunteers. Plunkett became director of military operations within the Brotherhood and other key positions were filled by Patrick Pearse and Thomas Mac-Donagh. Events began to move at a faster pace. The path to revolution became inevitable. The dramatic part played by Plunkett in that struggle sealed his tragic destiny.

NOTES

1. Oliver Plunkett was canonised in 1975. The ceremony in Rome was attended by both Catholic and Protestant members of the extended Plunkett family.
2. See article by Geraldine Plunkett Dillon published in the *University Review*, Vol.I, No.12, pp.36–45 in 1957.
3. *Idem.*
4. In 1900 Muckross Park was sold to the Dominican nuns, who set up schools there.
5. Information given to me by Blanaid O'Brolchain née Dillon, niece of Joseph Mary Plunkett.
6. See Geraldine Plunkett Dillon *op. cit.*
7. See Patricia Boylan *All Cultivated People*, p.69.
8. An interesting account of Plunkett and MacDonagh is contained in Chapter 13 of *Leaders and Men of the Easter Rising: Dublin 1916* edited by F. X. Martin (Methuen, 1967). The chapter was contributed by Donagh MacDonagh, the son of Thomas.
9. See Brendan Kennelly 'The Poetry of Joseph Plunkett' in the *Dublin Magazine*, Spring issue, 1966.
10. In England at the same time similar views were being expressed by Rupert Brooke, an icon of his generation who became one of the fatalities of the First World War.

CHAPTER THREE

The Love Story of Grace and Joseph

THE WRITER Katharine Tynan met Joe Plunkett as a young man and later recorded her impressions of him. He was 'a tall, delicate youth with something misty about him, very full of theories and with a somewhat opinionated air'.[1] There was also something theatrical about his appearance. He wore large rings and bracelets which he had acquired on trips abroad. His prosperous family background and his interest in literature and the theatre might have misled some to see him as something of a dilettante. Nothing could have been further from the truth. He was a serious young man with a mission in life. He used quite violent language in his political writing for the *Irish Review*. That weekly paper was suppressed in 1914 after he published 'Twenty Plain Facts for Irishmen' which was regarded by the authorities as inflammatory.

Although Joe had been a member of the United Arts Club where Grace was a frequent visitor, they did not meet each other there. Their first encounter was on the steps of St Enda's school when Mrs Dryhurst introduced them. No exact date is available but most sources place it as late 1914 or early 1915. It does not appear to have been love at first sight. Grace had many admirers and Joe had an earlier attachment to Columba O'Carroll, the daughter of a doctor who lived close to the home of the Plunketts in central Dublin. This romance was later described by Joe's sister Geraldine as a 'somewhat adolescent and unreal adoration of Columba' which was not reciprocated.[2] Their families had become well acquainted during two summer visits to an Irish College at Cloghaneely in County Donegal. Joe published *Sonnets to Columba* in 1913, having printed it on his hand-press. Such youthful 'crushes' are common and no doubt Joe had the resilience of youth to recover from it.

However, his deep, almost frenetic involvement in military matters now dominated his thoughts and activities. Although he was a very romantic young man, seeking a new love would not be a priority. One of his poems, 'Moriturus Te Salutat', probably refers to Columba:

> And yet I love you though you say
> You will not love me – truth is hard
> Twere so much easier to give way
> And stay the death-stroke, my reward –
> Courage, brave heart! tis Love you slay.[3]

It was Grace's interest in the Roman Catholic religion that led to the deepening of her acquaintance with Joe. She frequently visited the Pro-Cathedral in Dublin to hear the Palestrina choir (founded by Edward Martyn of Tulira in County Galway). The Pro-Cathedral was close to the poor areas of the inner city. Grace was deeply moved by the beautiful singing of the choir. She was touched, too, by the fervent devotion of the congregation there, particularly that shown by the women. Most of them were poorly dressed and visibly marked by the hardship of their lives. It was very different from the Church of the Holy Trinity in Rathmines where she had been taken by her Protestant mother throughout her childhood.[4] Rightly or wrongly, Grace believed that the prosperous congregation of Rathmines went there solely to display fine clothes and jewellery and to meet others of their social circle. She began to question Joe about his Catholic faith, a subject on which she could not have found a better teacher. A close friendship developed between them which ripened into romance.

At this time, Joe was deeply involved with the Volunteers. His mother allowed them to train in the grounds of Sandymount Castle and Larkfield in Kimmage, both of which were owned by the family. Eamon de Valera wrote to Joe in October 1914 to ask for his help in getting a hall for the winter months. In it, he referred to the generosity of the Countess in allowing the use of Sandymount Castle to his battalion.[5]

Roger Casement was sent to the United States of America in July 1914 to raise funds and support for the Volunteers. He was dismayed by the outbreak of World War I the following month. Like many people, Casement believed such a conflict would not happen for many years, if at all. He was critical of the policies of the British Foreign

27

Office that led to the outbreak of war and predicted that England would drag 'the whole world' into it. Casement hoped to protect the Irish people from becoming innocent victims in the struggle. Like Arthur Griffith and other patriots, he did not see Germany as an enemy or the cause of Ireland's ills. Later, Casement went to Germany to obtain support and arms for the Irish cause. In April 1915, Joe was sent to Berlin to help Casement in his efforts.

Joe made careful preparations for this mission. His sister Geraldine, with whom he was then sharing a house in Donnybrook, became a close confidante and assistant in the whole enterprise. With her, Joe arranged a code for messages he expected to send for delivery to Pearse or Sean MacDermott. As a precaution he destroyed all photographs of himself before he left. He grew a moustache and an imperial beard (fashionable at the time) to disguise his appearance. He decided to call himself 'James Malcolm' while he travelled. He was able to cover his departure as necessary for reasons of health. The secret nature of his journey and the elaborate precautions he took would have appealed to the theatrical side of his character. Joe passed through Spain, Italy and Switzerland before crossing the German frontier. He was anxious about the last stage of the journey as he could not speak German. He feared arrest as a British spy. However, this was avoided as a German agent escorted him to Berlin.

Joe found Casement in a sorry state. He was ill, miserable and very depressed. Always a highly-strung man, Casement was upset by the way he had been treated by the German High Command. There he was regarded with suspicion, partly due to warnings received from John Devoy, the Clan na Gael leader in the United States of America, who had not liked or trusted him. As Casement was not a member of the Irish Republican Brotherhood, the Germans wished to consult someone who was. Hence Joe Plunkett had been chosen as the necessary link in the chain. Joe did not like the visits to Irish prisoners of war in German camps, but he agreed to accompany Casement. Their attempt to get the young prisoners to return and fight in an Irish rising was doomed to failure. The men had already given their loyalty to Britain and believed that Home Rule would be established in Ireland when the war came to an end. They also saw Germany as the aggressor and instigator of the war, citing the fate of 'poor little Belgium'. In general, their attitude to Casement was hostile.

It was Joe who saw the German Chancellor, Bethmann-Hollweg, and negotiated with him. A cargo of arms and ammunition was promised, to arrive on Easter Sunday, 1916. Joe sent two messages home giving the outcome of his efforts. The first one never arrived. The second one, to his sister Geraldine in their pre-arranged code, got through. Casement had meanwhile become very concerned about Joe's health. He feared Joe might collapse at any time and said so in a letter to a German contact, a Mr Meyler.[6] Some sources suggest that Joe himself realised at this time he had not long to live. Notwithstanding he got back to Dublin safely, to Casement's relief. He attended the funeral of O'Donovan Rossa in August, an occasion best remembered for the stirring oration of Patrick Pearse at the graveside of the old Fenian. Joe was now working closely with Rory O'Connor and James Connolly on their plans for the rising. Both were impressed with his knowledge of military matters. That autumn Joe was sent to the United States of America to inform Clan na Gael of the progress being made in Ireland. While in New York he wrote to Grace's sister Sydney, there working as a journalist and propagandist for Ireland's claims. He asked Sydney to meet him and they had lunch together in a Turkish restaurant where they talked at length. At this time Joe and Grace were very friendly but not yet engaged to marry. Sydney found him looking very well. He told her he was a 'different man' since joining the Volunteers. He was relaxed and happy, which surprised her. Previously she had considered him taciturn and reserved, with little small talk. He told her nothing of the serious purpose of his visit and when they parted, left her with no idea of how long he expected to stay in the US.[7]

The writer Padraic Colum also met Joe in New York at this time. He and his wife Mary entertained the young revolutionary in their home and introduced him to other sympathisers with his cause. Colum was very impressed by his guest. Despite poor health, Joe's strong will and dedication were obvious.[8] On his return to Ireland, he continued with his deep involvement in military plans. He saw Grace as often as he could and by November the couple were deeply in love. On 2nd December he wrote to her ardently: 'I do love you. I hope to become more worthy of loving you. Will you marry me?'

A postscript to this letter explains his personal position:

By the way, I am actually a beggar. I have no income and am

earning nothing. Moreover there are other things more desperate, practically speaking, to prevent anyone marrying me.[9]

These 'other things' probably relate to his poor health and commitment to plans for an armed insurrection. Joe must have seen Grace that day as he wrote again to her in the evening:

> Darling Grace,
> You will marry me and nobody else. I have been a damned fool … but thank God I see. I love you and only you and will never love anyone else … I was never meant to be so happy. I can't believe what I know … I love you a million million times …

Grace did not tell her parents of her engagement as she knew they would not approve. She may have told some of her sisters, particularly Muriel who had married Thomas MacDonagh in 1912. Despite Isabella Gifford's dislike for the politics and religion of MacDonagh, his personal charm and kindness made him a favourite both with his mother-in-law and the family circle. The girls often enlisted his help in arguments with their mother, both on personal issues, such as smoking cigarettes, and on more serious matters. Among visitors to the Gifford home was a young lawyer called Kingsmill Moore,[10] who held strongly unionist political views. Grace often called on the help of MacDonagh in arguments with this guest.

A letter to Grace on 4th December expresses Joe's longing and the frustration he was feeling:

> It seems awfully silly that we should not be able to be together all the time and especially at the end of the day and all through the lovely hours of the quiet night. I want to hold you close and feel your happiness that is mine … you have taken the harm out of all my troubles and made the whole world beautiful for me. You have made me happy – never forget that whatever happens because it's a kind of miracle.

Six days later, another letter shows a more humourous side of Joe's nature:

> Well, I heard what was supposed to be a very absurd story about you and me being engaged. I said 'Yes, wasn't it and the funny

part is that Grace believes it too!' Listen, will you make up a lovely screed for the announcement, saying who we are etc. Of course, it should be done by your mother!

It was Sean MacDermott, then working closely with Joe, who had questioned him about the 'absurd story'. Among other friends who congratulated Joe were Shane Lester[11] and Padraic O'Riain. By Christmas the engagement was well-known to close friends of the couple. Grace had decided to take instruction in the Catholic religion as a preparation for the marriage. Joe wrote continuously to her, sometimes from Larkfield in Kimmage where he was spending a lot of time. On St Stephen's Day he wrote:

> It's awful to be without you – you know if I was only coming home to you after my work it would be different.

Grace often went to Larkfield to visit Joe. Early in February he was confined to bed with a cold which persisted for weeks. The weather was snowy which did not help his recovery. If Joe realised how seriously ill he was, he never told Grace. Later in life, she wrote that all she knew with certainty was that he had problems with the glands in his neck.[12] In fact, Joe had advanced tuberculosis. His sister, Geraldine, who had always tried to look after his health, believed he was dying and he had known this since his visit to Germany the previous year.[13] Earlier references to his 'tendency to pleurisy' may have been euphemistic. At the time, tuberculosis was often concealed by the relatives of the victim for fear of damage to the whole family if revealed. This attitude persisted for a long time. In spite of everything, it is quite possible that Joe hoped he would survive. Tuberculosis is not an illness that depresses the patient. In fact, the slight fever that accompanies it is often a source of buoyancy.

The *Irish Life* magazine on 11th February published an announcement of the engagement in the formal manner of the time:

> An engagement is announced between Mr Joseph Mary Plunkett, 26 Fitzwilliam Street Upper, eldest son of Count Plunkett Director of the National Museum, Kildare Street, and Miss Grace Gifford, daughter of Mr Frederick Gifford, 8 Temple Villas, Palmerston Park, Dublin.[14]

Joe had suggested to Grace that they might marry during Lent but she thought Easter would be preferable. Grace was formally received into the Catholic Church on 7th April at the University Church on St Stephen's Green. The priest who officiated was Father James Sherwin (later Archdeacon). No official record survives of who her sponsors were but Joe's sister Fiona was one of them. Perhaps Fiona was the only sponsor, although the custom was to have two. Father Sherwin, a friend of Count Plunkett, probably helped in making the necessary arrangements for his son's fiancée.

Throughout her life, Grace kept a postcard photograph of the interior of University Church. A note on the back identifies it as 'the Church where I was baptised on 7-4-1916'.[15] Joe gave Grace a special poem he composed for the occasion. The second verse is as follows:

> The joy of Spring leaps from your eyes
> The strength of dragons from your hair,
> In your young soul we still surprise
> The secret wisdom flowing there
> But never word shall speak or sing
> Inadequate music where above
> Your burning heart now spreads its wing
> In the wild beauty of your Love.

This day was a very happy one for Grace. She had formally become a Catholic, a step she had long wished to take. Everything was now in order and she could complete her plans for the wedding, due to take place on Easter Sunday, 23rd April. She was not fully aware of the detailed military plans Joe was making and indeed, as a member of the oath-bound Irish Republican Brotherhood, he could not have told her about them. Grace was a strong nationalist and a staunch supporter of Sinn Féin but she was not politically involved beyond that. She never joined Cumann na mBan, the women's auxiliary organisation that worked to support the Irish Volunteers although Joe had suggested she might. As the fateful final weeks before Easter passed, she did not realise how the coming revolution was to disrupt her life and her hopes of personal happiness.

NOTES

1. See Chapter 9 of Katharine Tynan, *The Years of the Shadow*, published in 1919.
2. See Geraldine Plunkett Dillon article in the *University Review*, Vol.I, No.12, pp.36–45, 1957.
3. See *The Poems of Joseph Mary Plunkett* (Talbot Press, Dublin, 1917).
4. Grace had been christened there on 8th August, 1888. She was given the names Grace Eveleen.
5. The original letter was shown to me by Ann Burke.
6. This pencil note is included in Ms. 10,999 in the National Library with other papers in the Josephine Plunkett collection.
7. See Sydney Gifford Czira, *The Years Flew By*, p.78.
8. See *The Irish Rebellion of 1916 and its Martyrs* by Colum and other (New York, 1916). Chapter XXIII, pp.413–16 deals with Plunkett.
9. Grace kept the love letters Joe wrote to her between November 1915 and Easter 1916. They are now in the National Library, Ms. 21,590.
10. Kingsmill Moore later became a High Court judge.
11. Shane Lester (later called Sean) joined the Department of External Affairs in 1922. He later became Secretary-General of the League of Nations.
12. See Ms. 21,598 in the National Library.
13. See her article in the *Dublin Magazine* for Spring 1966.
14. The custom then was not to mention the mothers.
15. Ms. 21,591 in the National Library.

CHAPTER FOUR

The Easter Rising

THE FULL STORY of the Easter Rising has been told many times. It had many unusual features. Revolutions seldom originate directly from academics or writers or are led by them. The 1916 leaders were seen as 'obscure cranks' by those who supported the establishment of rule by Britain and Dublin Castle. The direct involvement of Plunkett was also seen as unlikely; he was out of his class in the movement because of his social background among the landed aristocracy. However, Joe's father, Count Plunkett, supported his son's political views. Despite his earlier efforts in contesting elections between 1891 and 1898, the Count had never been elected to the British parliament. On each occasion he had been defeated by unionists. The Count followed political events closely and by 1915 his own views had become more republican and revolutionary. In that year he is said to have joined the Irish Republican Brotherhood, taking the oath from his eldest son, Joseph. His younger sons, George and Jack, also involved themselves in the movement by training young recruits at Larkfield as Volunteers and helping their eldest brother in other ways.

Grace often went to Larkfield to see her fiancé and she helped Joe to transcribe the famous document that became public on 19th April. This document was in code and was said to have been leaked from Dublin Castle by a civil servant there, Eugene Smith, who supported the nationalist cause.[1] The document was published by Joe with the aim of gaining widespread support for the insurrection. It reported that orders had been given to disarm the Irish Volunteers and to arrest most of the leaders. The code was deciphered by Joe while Grace wrote it down. It was then set up on a hand-press at Larkfield by Colm O'Lochlainn and George Plunkett. The document became public when read to a meeting of Dublin Corporation by Alderman Tom Kelly. It was immediately denounced as 'bogus' by the British government. Some nationalists also believed that Joe had forged the document and understood his reasons, even if they did not agree with his strategy. More recently, it is generally considered to be a 'material forgery' although there is still some controversy about it.[2]

As far as Grace was concerned, the document was genuine and she defended it all her life.[3] Her sister Sydney also believed that Joe would not have been capable of such a deception.[4] In those last weeks before Easter, the pace of events quickened. Apart from military plans, the final wording of the Proclamation of the Republic was agreed and signed by six of the leaders in the home of Jennie Wyse Power at 21, Henry Street in the centre of Dublin.[5] Pearse, Clarke, Connolly, Mac-Donagh, MacDermott and Ceannt signed on that occasion, while Joe Plunkett signed it afterwards on the morning of Easter Monday.

Shortly before Easter Joe went into a nursing home to have another operation on the glands of his neck. Grace visited him there and they discussed their plans for the immediate future. It was then that Joe told her he wished their wedding to go ahead even if he was in jail. He left the nursing home on Saturday 23rd April and stayed that night in the Metropole Hotel. Grace visited him that evening. Earlier that day, Michael Collins had called to her home to give her some money from Joe and a small gun for her protection. Later in life she wrote that she did not know whether the gun or the money frightened her more. On Easter Sunday Joe made a will in which he left everything to Grace. The only witness was his younger brother George. At nine o'clock that evening Joe wrote to Grace:

> My dearest heart,
> Keep up your spirits and trust in Providence. Everything is bully.
> I have only a minute. I am going into the nursing home to-night
> to sleep. I am keeping as well as anything but need a rest. Take
> care of your old cold, sweetheart.
> All my love for ever,
> Joe

In that last week before Easter, Eoin MacNeill, Chief-of-Staff of the Irish Volunteers, had learned of the secret plans for the rising made by the military council of the Irish Republican Brotherhood. MacNeill had opposed the idea of an armed insurrection on the grounds that it would not succeed. When he learned of this deception on Thursday, he was naturally very angry and told his informants he would do everything in his power, short of informing the government, to prevent the rising. On Good Friday, three visitors called to MacNeill's home in an attempt to persuade him to change his mind. They were Patrick Pearse, Sean MacDermott and Thomas MacDonagh. MacNeill was told that arms from Germany were on the way and that the rising would go ahead whether he opposed it or not. With some reluctance MacNeill finally agreed to support the plans. Later he changed his mind. Hearing of the arrest, in Kerry, of Roger Casement and the loss of the German arms, he decided to countermand the order he had already given for the mobilisation of all the Volunteers on Easter Sunday. A notice to that effect appeared in the *Irish Independent* newspaper and copies were sent to branches of the Volunteers all over the country. The confusion caused by this change on MacNeill's part forced the military leaders to postpone the date of the Rising until Easter Monday. This explains why only a few of the country branches rose in support. There simply was not time to pass on Pearse's order to go ahead to the scattered branches.

On Easter Monday morning Joe joined the group of Volunteers at Liberty Hall who planned, with James Connolly and his Citizen Army, to seize the General Post Office and other buildings in the city. Shortly before noon, James Connolly led them out, attired in his uniform and polished leggings. On his right marched Patrick Pearse, showing his dignified bearing as he went to take his place in the long-awaited hour. On Connolly's left walked Joe Plunkett, his throat still swathed in bandages. He had dressed carefully in his uniform and carried a sword. His hands were covered with rings, part of his flamboyant appearance for years. He had taken his sabre out of its sheath before the group advanced. Thomas Clarke, Sean MacDermott and Sean T. O'Kelly were marching behind, as was Winifred Carney of the Citizen's Army. She was to spend the following six days in the General Post Office. Other women there were members of Cumann na mBan who took no part in the fighting but worked to feed the garrison, nurse the wounded and carry despatches. Countess Markievicz was part of the Citizen Army contingent that fought under Michael Mallin in St Stephen's Green and the College of Surgeons. Fifteen women of the Citizen Army were in that group, including Grace's sister Nellie who took charge of the cooking, a task for which she was well qualified. Grace later wrote that she had not known of Nellie's membership of the Citizen Army or of her plans to take part in the insurrection.

When the group arrived in the General Post Office it met with no resistance. Both staff and customers scattered quickly. Two flags were soon raised over the building. One was green with a harp in the centre and bore the word 'Irish Republic' in gold and white Irish lettering. The other was the tricolour of green, white and orange which later became the official national flag. Pearse read the proclamation in front of the building to the random group gathered there. Reaction was very different from that anticipated. Pearse was used to addressing sympathetic listeners. A mixture of incredulity, amusement and hostility was the response. Plainly no real support was there for Pearse and his comrades-in-arms. James Connolly, who watched the scene, was deeply moved. He took Pearse's hand with the words 'Thanks be to God, Pearse, that we have lived to see this day'.

As has often been pointed out, Pearse was a most unlikely leader of a revolution. Essentially a man of thought, he lacked practical skills and was to spend most of his time that Easter week writing at a table. Connolly and O'Rahilly were more realistic, as was Michael Collins who quickly proved himself to be the most efficient officer in the building. Also there were Desmond Fitzgerald[6] and his wife Mabel. Fitzgerald had been born and reared in London but after a visit to Kerry, where his mother had lived her early life, he became deeply attached to that 'western brink' of Europe. After his marriage to Mabel McConnell he lived first in France but in 1913 moved to Kerry. He joined both the Volunteers and the Irish Republican Brotherhood. Mabel, who came from a northern unionist background, had become an ardent republican and supported her husband's participation in the armed struggle. Later in life, Desmond Fitzgerald wrote his memoirs.[7] The chapter written about Easter week in the General Post Office is a valuable record, with many references to Joseph Plunkett. Clearly Joe was too ill to take part in the fighting. Indeed, he lay most of the time on an improvised bed where food was brought to him. Fitzgerald was in charge of food supplies and was helped in this task by Peggy Downey. She was an Irish girl on holiday from Liverpool who had offered her services to the cause. She estimated their supplies could feed two hundred men for three weeks. Pearse had given orders to economise so the food would last.

Fitzgerald recorded that he talked to Plunkett almost every time he was in the big hall on the ground floor. Pearse sometimes joined them, as did O'Rahilly. Fitzgerald felt great pity for Plunkett whom he considered to be a dying man. He admired his cheerful spirits and how Plunkett could forget their ill-fated position when in animated conversation. They discussed literature and mutual friends. More seriously they discussed the 'moral rectitude' of their present actions, quoting every theological argument in support of them. Fitzgerald believed they were all going to die. Personally he dreaded the possibility of being hanged but the general opinion was that they would face a soldier's death by firing squad. Plunkett told Fitzgerald the story of his visit to Germany and its limited success; in the end, the authorities there had sent only arms for which they had been paid. They also discussed the possibility of an independent Ireland with a German prince as titular head until full freedom was a reality. As the week wore on with increased bombardment Pearse joined Plunkett and Fitzgerald and discussed plans to evacuate the building. They decided that the women should be asked to leave before the surrender. In the end, the women agreed to this apart from Louise Gavan Duffy, who had worked tirelessly as cook, and Peggy Downey. They insisted on staying.

Inside the General Post Office there was a mixture of efficiency and chaos. O'Rahilly, who joined the insurgents at the last minute despite his personal misgivings about the whole enterprise, proved a valuable officer. He saw that the upper floor of the building was properly fortified. At times everything ran short and groups were sent out to commandeer food, bedding and medical supplies. Desmond Fitzgerald, adjutant to O'Rahilly, was sent out to pay cash for these extras, as shopkeepers were reluctant to accept receipts with a promise of repayment by the Irish Republic.

In the early part of that week, Grace's sister Muriel, whose husband Thomas MacDonagh was in command at Jacob's biscuit factory, called into the General Post Office. She talked to Plunkett who told her he wanted his wedding to go ahead even in prison. The burden of anxiety endured by Muriel and Grace throughout the week is almost impossible to describe or even imagine. Both knew military defeat was inevitable. Although they hoped, as did many others, the insurgents would be treated as prisoners of war they could not feel sure of such an outcome. Grace spent a lot of time with Muriel, who lived close to their parents' home in Rathmines. Muriel's home then was 29, Oakley Road, Ranelagh. Eamonn Ceannt's wife was also staying. Her husband was in command at the South Dublin Union building. There was little or nothing they could do except wait, pray and hope.

Meanwhile, within the General Post Office, Joe was exerting himself to help restore order. Pearse, exhausted after six days with little or no sleep, had temporarily lost his composure. The whole building was on fire and it was clear that evacuation could not be delayed. This was on Friday evening. Joe again showed great courage despite his illness. He called on the men to be brave as they marched into the hail of bullets in Henry Street. They found a temporary refuge in Cogan's shop at 30, Moore Street. Thomas Clarke and Sean MacDermott were already there and James Connolly arrived later. Mrs Cogan, who, like many families in the area was sympathetic to the insurgent, fed all her uninvited guests.

Both Plunkett and Connolly suffered physically from the rigours of the withdrawal. Connolly had been wounded with what proved to be a compound fracture of the leg. Some of the group hoped to escape capture despite the fact that British troops were all around them. Joe snatched a quiet moment to send a brief note to Grace: 'I have made my deeds as right as I could see and make them and cannot wish them undone.'[8]

Following Pearse's order to surrender, little option remained to those trapped in Moore Street. Connolly's wound had turned gangrenous and it was clear he could not be moved. Pearse had joined the group in the shop. Seeing clearly that they would have to surrender, some of them knelt together to say the Rosary, as Nurse Julia Grenan later recorded. Carrying the wounded, they moved to 16, Moore Street. It was from that house they marched out, led by Willie Pearse who carried a white flag. They walked to the Parnell monument in O'Connell Street where they handed over their arms. They were then taken to the forecourt of the Rotunda Hospital, where they spent the night. This experience was an extra hardship for Plunkett and Connolly. Sean MacDermott, who had a limp since an attack of polio in 1912, had to march without his customary stick which a British officer had taken from him. From the Rotunda, Patrick Pearse was taken to solitary confinement in Arbour Hill detention barracks. Plunkett, together with other leaders and men, was taken to Richmond Barracks. James Connolly was brought to the infirmary in Dublin Castle.

Meanwhile, other commandants in their various buildings were reluctant to accept the order to surrender. Eamon de Valera refused to obey the order unless it was endorsed by his superior officer, Thomas MacDonagh. The latter had several reasons for hesitation before accepting the order. He feared Pearse had been taken prisoner and was under duress to make it. He also thought he and his men could hold out much longer. He insisted on being brought to General Lowe, who received him courteously. He agreed to give MacDonagh time to consult the other commandants and safe conduct while this was done. When he returned to Jacob's factory he told his men that 'one glorious week' had achieved their aim, bursting into tears as he did so. Then, still very upset, he left to consult Eamonn Ceannt in the South Dublin Union. Jointly they decided to surrender. By this time Eamon de Valera's difficulty had been resolved. Nurse Elizabeth O'Farrell had obtained MacDonagh's signature and brought it back to Boland's Mill. De Valera, MacDonagh, Ceannt and the remaining commandants all surrendered by Sunday 30th April. The Rising had lasted for six whole days, long enough to impress the world outside and to shake British power in Ireland for ever.

NOTES

1. His daughter later married Donagh MacDonagh.
2. See Chapters 11 and 13 in *Leaders and Men of the Easter Rising: Dublin 1916*, edited by F. X. Martin (Methuen, London, 1967).
3. See Ms. 21,598 in NLI. This is a statement for the Military History Bureau completed by Grace in June 1949.
4. See Sydney Gifford Czira *The Years Flew By*, p.28.
5. For a full account of the life of this remarkable woman see *From Parnell to De Valera* by Marie O'Neill (Blackwater Press, Dublin, 1991). The house in Henry Street is now marked by a handsome plaque, the work of Cliona Cussen.
6. Desmond Fitzgerald supported the treaty. He became Minister for External Affairs from 1922–1927 and Minister for Defence from 1927–1932. He was the father of Dr Garrett Fitzgerald who headed two coalition governments between 1982 and 1987.
7. Published posthumously in 1968.
8. See Ms. 21,594 in NLI.

CHAPTER FIVE

The Prison Wedding

FOLLOWING the surrender Plunkett, together with other leaders
and men, was taken to Richmond barracks. There they awaited
their fate. Conditions in the barracks were crowded and uncomfort-
able. Liam O'Briain, who had fought in St Stephen's Green and the
College of Surgeons under the command of Michael Mallin and
Countess Markievicz, was also among the prisoners there. Later in his
life he described the scene:

> My best friend Sean MacDermott was there – poor, lame Sean,
> affectionate, gay, handsome, warm-hearted. The first thing he
> said to me was 'What's that you have under your arm?' It was the
> old quilt I had brought with me from the College of Surgeons.
> 'Give it to Plunkett' he said 'he is very sick'. Joe Plunkett was
> lying on the floor near him, trying and failing to rest. For a couple
> of days following he had the old quilt, sometimes under him as a
> bed, sometimes under his head as a pillow. Plunkett was wearing
> his Volunteer uniform and top boots, as were his two brothers,
> George and Sean ...[1]

General Maxwell, the Commander-in-Chief of the British forces in
Ireland, made arrangements for the courts-martial of the prisoners.
Knowing little of Irish history, he had no sympathy at all for the
'rebels'. He was determined to give the leaders in particular what he
saw as rapid and stern justice. Brigadier-General Blackadder, who
presided at the courts-martial, was a man of a different disposition. He
found his role a very depressing experience. Dining with some friends
on the evening after Patrick Pearse's summary trial, he explained his
feelings:

> I have just done one of the hardest tasks I have ever had to do. I

41

have had to condemn to death one of the finest characters I have ever come across. There must be something very wrong in the state of things, that makes a man like that a rebel.[2]

Pearse had been kept in solitary confinement in Arbour Hill until the Tuesday after the surrender. He was then taken to Richmond Barracks for his court-martial. Thomas Clarke and Thomas MacDonagh were tried on the same morning. All three were condemned to death by firing squad. They were transferred to Kilmainham jail where the executions were carried out at 3.30 am on 3rd May. Plunkett had also been tried at Richmond barracks, condemned to death and transferred to Kilmainham jail to await his execution. Records of the courts-martial are not available at the present time.[3] Brigadier-General Blackadder later said that all the men he had tried behaved well. He singled out Major John MacBride as the most soldierly in his bearing.[4]

The agony of mind which Grace suffered is almost impossible to describe. With her sister Muriel she waited helplessly as the fates of her fiancé and her brother-in-law were decided. However, knowing the wishes of Joe that the wedding should go ahead, she made some preparations. Many relatives of the leaders and men had clung to the hope that their loved ones would be treated as prisoners-of-war. This proved as mistaken as the belief of James Connolly that the insurgents could hold out for a longer period because the British forces would not destroy the occupied buildings. When Grace knew that Joe was due to be shot on 4th May, she bought the wedding ring at a jewellery shop in Grafton Street, in the city centre. The time was late afternoon on Wednesday 3rd May. Mr Stoker, who sold the ring to Grace, later described the circumstances. He had been about to close the shop when 'a young and attractive lady, evidently of good social position' came in and asked to be shown some wedding rings. He noticed that, despite the veil she wore, it was plain to see that her eyes were red from weeping. As she spoke, she tried to stifle convulsive sobs. Surprised by her distress, Mr Stoker asked her what was the trouble. 'You should not cry when you are going to be married' he said to her. Grace hesitated for a moment. Then, with tears running down her cheeks, she told him that she was 'Mr Plunkett's fiancée' and that she was to marry him that night before his execution the next morning. Mr Stoker, obviously a kindly man, tried to express his sympathy. Grace thanked him 'very quietly', chose the most expensive ring and paid for it in notes. She then left the shop.[5]

The weather all that week was very warm, more like June than early May. Grace wore a light frock made of a check fabric with white collar and cuffs. She also wore a light hat with a brim. It had been arranged by Joe that the prison chaplain, Father Eugene MacCarthy, would perform the ceremony. The wedding has often been described. Here are Grace's own words:

> I entered Kilmainham Jail on Wednesday 3rd May at 6 pm and was detained there till about 11.30 pm when I saw him (i.e. Joe) for the first time in the prison chapel where the marriage was gone through and no speeches allowed. He was taken back to his cell and I left the prison with Father Eugene MacCarthy of James's Street. We tried to get shelter for the night and I was finally lodged at the house of Mr Byrne – bell-founder – in James's Street. I went to bed at 1.30 and was wakened at 2 o'clock by a policeman, with a letter from the prison commandant – Major Lennon – asking me to visit Joseph Plunkett. I was brought there in a motor and saw my husband in his cell, the interview occupying 10 minutes. During the interview the cell was packed with officers, and a sergeant, who kept a watch in his hand and closed the interview by saying 'Your time is now up'.[6]

Plunkett had been placed at first in the infirmary of the jail, in a small cell with a plank bed and one blanket. There he was left without a light. Later he was moved to one of the cells close to those occupied by his comrades-in-arms. For the wedding, he was led to the chapel in handcuffs, which were removed for the ceremony and put on afterwards when he was marched away. The chapel was in darkness but one soldier held a lighted candle. Two soldiers acted as witnesses.[7] Grace's final meeting with her husband was spoiled because the cell was crowded. She later said:

> We who had never had enough time to say what we wanted to each other found that in that last ten minutes we couldn't talk at all.[8]

43

Plunkett was executed at 3.30 am on 4th May. Four Capuchin priests from Church Street had been summoned to give spiritual help to him, Willie Pearse, Edward Daly and Michael O'Hanrahan who were also awaiting execution. Father Albert was one of the four. He noticed Plunkett and looked at him with particular interest. Their eye met and Joe walked across the room to talk to him: 'Father, I want you to know that I am dying for the glory of God and the honour of Ireland.'[9] These sentiments were repeated by Plunkett as he waited with his hands tied behind his back to be led to the execution yard. To Father Sebastian, the Capuchin who waited with him, he said he was very happy because he was dying for his faith and his country.[10] A few minutes later, Plunkett and his three companions were dead. It was only five days since they had surrendered.

After Grace had seen her husband for the last time she was driven to the home of her sister, Katie Wilson, on the north side of the city.[11] It was usually said that Grace's parents refused to allow her home after her marriage but this statement may be too strong. Certainly her mother, interviewed by a journalist shortly afterwards, was very unsympathetic. She told of hearing of Grace's engagement but had not discussed it with her because she disapproved of the match. Knowing of their developing friendship, she had earlier warned Grace that marriage to Joe Plunkett would be 'a very foolish thing', but Grace had defied her mother. Mrs Gifford added: 'She was always a very headstrong and self-willed girl and had lived a more or less independent life for some time.'[12]

Some allowance must be made for the fact that Grace's mother was very upset at the time. Her husband Frederick had just suffered a stroke and was being cared for in their home. She had never approved of Joe Plunkett's religion or his politics and had equally disliked those of her son-in-law, Thomas MacDonagh. MacDonagh, however, had been given the time in which to charm his wife's mother and she had become fond of him. Muriel was a very gentle and sweet person and more of a favourite with her mother than Grace. Widowed and virtually penniless, with two young children to rear on her own, Muriel's tragedy may have been more of a concern for her mother than Grace's. Knowing this, Grace probably did not wish to return to her parents' home. The support and friendship of her sisters was to be vital for her in the years ahead, as well as in the immediate aftermath of her bereavement.

The prison wedding was briefly announced in the *Irish Times* newspaper on 7th May: 'May 3rd, 1916 at Dublin Joseph Plunkett to Grace Gifford.'

In the immediate period after the Rising, an enormous number of people suspected of either involvement or sympathy with the 'rebels' were arrested and imprisoned. Included were Count Plunkett and his wife Josephine who were subsequently ordered to leave Ireland. Early in June they were released from jail in Dublin to attend a Requiem Mass for their son at the Carmelite Church at Whitefriar Street in the city. Grace was present, together with Joe's sister Geraldine who was now married to Thomas Dillon. The large attendance was duly reported in the newspapers. In the immediate aftermath of the Rising, Grace moved for a while to the Plunkett family home at Larkfield. It was during this time that Grace suffered a miscarriage, according to her sister-in-law Geraldine Dillon. While there have always been rumours that Grace was pregnant at the time of her marriage, until recently there was no source to support such a story. The newly available data is contained in the papers of Geraldine Dillon in the manuscripts department of the National Library of Ireland. These papers include drafts of Geraldine's unpublished memoirs of her long life and deal in particular with the events of 1916 and the part played by her brother, Joseph Mary, in that struggle. Geraldine was undoubtedly in a position to know the facts about Grace's life in the period immediately after the Rising and there is no reason to doubt her honesty in recording the miscarriage. However, some of her other statements are open to doubt. Having said that she did not discuss the pregnancy and miscarriage with Grace at the time, she goes on to suggest that Joseph might not have been the father of the child, citing an unknown source in the following words: 'The Castle version was that she [i.e. Grace] was pregnant but that Joe was not the father. I thought either case was possible.'

Geraldine states that she got on well with Grace who had 'many good qualities'. Nevertheless, the tone of her memoir is hostile to Grace, portrayed as an immoral girl (by the standards of the period) and motivated mainly by greed in her engagement and marriage. Geraldine died in 1986. She was about ninety-five years old. During her lifetime she had never written or spoken publicly about Grace's pregnancy. We may wonder why, in her old age, she broke her silence.

In doing so she showed rancour towards Grace who had been dead for many years. Perhaps she had remained silent to protect the memory of her brother. In such a puritanical period people were intolerant of anyone who breached the code of sexual morals. In her later years, however, she may have felt that the truth should be told, whatever the cost.

It seems unlikely that another man was responsible for Grace's condition. If Joseph was not the father (and assuming he knew this), we can only speculate about his motives for marrying Grace. Were they purely quixotic, to protect her and save her reputation? Did he want to save her from a forced marriage to someone chosen by her mother, as Geraldine suggests? Given that Joe was passionately in love with Grace, as shown in his ardent letters to her, and the couple had been formally engaged to marry since Christmas of 1915, such a scenario seems improbable. Unless further evidence on these intimate matters comes to light in the future, it seems reasonable to assume that Joseph was the father of Grace's expected child.

One of his poems, published after his death, may refer to his relationship with Grace. The title was 'New Love':

> The day I knew you loved me we had lain
> Deep in Coill Doraca down by Gleann na Scath
> Unknown to each till suddenly I saw
> You in the shadow, knew oppressive pain
> Stopping my heart, and there you did remain
> In dreadful beauty fair without a flaw,
> Blinding the eyes that yet could not withdraw
> Till wild between us drove the wind and rain.
>
> Breathless we reached the brugh before the west
> Burst in full fury – then with lightning stroke
> The tempest in my heart roared up and broke
> Its barriers, and I swore I would not rest
> Till that mad heart was worthy of your breast
> Or dead for you – and then this love awoke.

The last line obscures the meaning of the verses. Was it all a dream or some kind of mystic experience?

While Grace was staying at Larkfield she was interviewed by an American journalist, Eileen Moore, for an article, subsequently published in early October by a Chicago newspaper *The New World*. The writer, deeply impressed by Grace, wrote warmly of her beauty, charm and courage.

Meanwhile, public opinion in Ireland had changed dramatically. The initial hostility to the leaders and men who had taken part in the insurrection diminished. The summary trials and rapid executions of the leaders stunned the country. As curt military announcements of execution were issued day after day, giving the names of the men, public anger grew. Joe Plunkett, clearly a very sick man, had been shot while sitting in a chair as he was too ill to stand. This caused particular revulsion, as did the circumstances of the seriously wounded James Connolly. People expressed reluctant admiration for the leaders who had fought bravely for their cause. This soon swelled to the belief that the insurgents had been right.

The member of parliament, John Dillon, was in Dublin during Easter week. He wrote to his parliamentary party leader John Redmond on 30th April with some anxiety:

> You should urge strongly on the government the *extreme* unwisdom of any wholesale shooting of prisoners. The wisest course is to execute *no one* for the present ... If there were shootings of prisoners on a large scale the effect on public opinion might be disastrous in the extreme. So *far* feeling of the population in Dublin is *against* the Sinn Féiners. But a reaction might very easily be created.

John Redmond, more remote from the situation and still in London, did not respond quickly to Dillon's prophetic warning. Earlier, he had denounced the Rising in the House of Commons. However, as the rapid executions continued he too became anxious. He put pressure on Prime Minister Herbert Asquith to stop them. Asquith, inevitably pre-occupied by the European war, was slow to act on Ireland. He sent an indirect and weak message to General Maxwell to the effect that he was 'surprised and perturbed' at the shooting of so many 'rebel' leaders. In general, Asquith, like most English people, saw the Rising as an unjustified stab-in-the-back. Moreover, casualties had been high.

A total of three hundred had been killed, of which one hundred and eighty were insurgents or civilians and rest army and police personnel. Almost a thousand people had been wounded.[13] However, public opinion asserted itself in the way Dillon had predicted and a change of policy came about. Sadly it was too late to save James Connolly and Sean MacDermott, the last signatories of the Proclamation who were shot on 12th May. The death sentences on Eamon de Valera and Thomas Ashe, both surviving commandants of the Rising, were commuted to penal servitude for life.

Some time after Plunkett's execution, Dr L. F. Rowan, medical officer in County Kildare, wrote to an Irish newspaper stating that he had returned to Countess Plunkett the hat worn by her son while he waited to receive the volley of the firing squad. The hat had been given to the doctor by a British sergeant who witnessed the execution. He told the doctor that a soldier had removed from Plunkett's body rosary beads and the Volunteer hat. The sergeant, who wished to remain anonymous, retrieved both items and put the rosary beads on Plunkett's body. Feeling unable to return the hat to the Plunkett family, he asked the doctor to do so.[14]

A few days after Plunkett's death, Wilfred Maynell, a distinguished English writer sympathetic to Ireland's aspirations for political independence, wrote a poem in memory of Joseph. Maynell, a devout Catholic, wrote regularly on religious matters. He noticed that Joseph Plunkett had signed the Proclamation omitting his second name, Mary:

> Because you left her name unnamed,
> Lest some should surely think it shamed,
> I, with a bolder pen in rhyme,
> Link Joseph Mary all the time.
>
> I think, although you were not due
> She waited at the gate for you,
> And wore a sweet celestial pout
> Because her name had been left out.
>
> For this is very She who sings:
> 'The poor God filleth with good things'
> And Rebel She, who dares to say
> 'But empty sends the rich away'.

Later in her life, Grace wrote her own short poem on the 1916 leaders:

> Little we thought who watched your strength and power
> That you would lie 'defeated' 'neath the sod;
> The flag is furled that knew your glorious hour,
> Your eyes are closed now by the hand of God.
> (And yet from age to age remember we
> Christ did not die in vain on Calvary).

The story of the prison wedding, seized on by the newspapers, was reported all over the world. The writer and scholar Walter Starkie, who was from a Unionist background, later wrote that anecdotes about the ill-fated bride and groom fanned the fire of indignation growing in Ireland. Grace became a tragic symbol, like Sarah Curran, the beloved of Robert Emmet, in an earlier time.[15] Many people regarded the aims of 1916 as a lost cause. This was far from the truth. Grace played her part in the continuing struggle, as did her father-in-law, Count Plunkett, and other members of both the Plunkett and Gifford families.

NOTES

1. See Liam O'Briain 'Cuimhri Cinn' pp.151–2. O'Briain subsequently became Professor of Romance Languages in University College, Galway.
2. See *Seventy Years Young*, the memoirs of Elizabeth, Countess of Fingall p.376. First published in 1937, a paperback edition was issued in 1991 by Lilliput Press, Dublin.
3. I understand they are not to be released until the year 2016.
4. See Leon O'Broin *W. E. Wylie and the Irish Revolution* pp.26–7 (Gill and Macmillan, 1989).
5. See Ms. 21,593 in the National Library. Mr Stoker's statement was published in *Lloyd's Weekly News* on 7th May.
6. This account is taken from Ms. 21,593 in the National Library. The wedding was also described in R. M. Fox's *Rebel Irishwoman* pp.76–7 (Talbot Press, Dublin, 1935) and in the statement Grace gave to the Military History Bureau in 1949. The letter from Major Lennon is among the exhibits in Kilmainham Jail, now a museum.
7. It has been stated that only one soldier acted as a witness. The marriage certificate gives the names of John Smith and John Carberry as witnesses.

Father Eugene MacCarthy signed as both celebrant and witness.

8. See R.M. Fox *Rebel Irishwomen* pp.75–89.
9. See the *Capuchin Annual* 1942 p.453 for a short article written by Josephine Plunkett about her son.
10. See Sydney Gifford Czira *The Years Flew By* p.29.
11. Katie was a linguist and graduate of the Royal University. Prior to the Treaty she worked for Michael Collins on the Republican Bonds scheme.
12. See article 'Mrs Gifford's Story' published in *Lloyd's Weekly News* on 7th May. Some sources suggest it was Plunkett's poor health which caused Isabella Gifford's objections to the marriage. See letter to the *Irish Times* sent by Sydney Czira which was published on 21st April, 1966.
13. These figures are taken from the *Sinn Féin Rebellion Handbooks* published by the *Irish Times* in 1916 and 1917.
14. The hat and other mementoes of Plunkett were later given to the National Museum. The doctor's letter is among newspaper cuttings in Ms. 21,595 in the National Library.
15. See Walter Starkie's autobiography *Scholars and Gypsies* p.153 (John Murray, London, 1963).

The Struggle Continues

A FTER THE RISING and its immediate aftermath, the rest of the year 1916 passed quietly in Ireland. The country, stunned by the whole trauma, took some time to recover. The surviving leaders were held in British jails, limiting the chances of further political activities. Public opinion in Britain, to some extent, had become uneasy and critical of the drastic military response to events in Ireland. It was thought to be unacceptable to keep so many Irishmen in prison – especially those who had taken no part in the fighting. Arthur Griffith was released just before Christmas. Although his policy had been one of passive resistance, he had offered to fight in the Rising when he knew it was a certainty. He was persuaded that he was more useful to the cause as a writer and propagandist. When released, he was regarded as a very important and influential figure. The British authorities dub-bed the Rising the 'Sinn Féin Rebellion'. This was incorrect but to some degree understandable; so many Sinn Féin members were also Volunteers and some of them were also members of the Irish Repub-lican Brotherhood. Moreover, the separatist policies of Sinn Féin had been well-known to the government for years. After 1916, belief in Griffith's policies became widespread in Ireland. Many people now considered that abstention from the Westminster parliament was the best course.

Grace decided to devote herself through her art to the promotion of Sinn Féin policies. She resumed her commercial work to earn her living. Drawing for advertisements gave her a small income but her financial position was very precarious. In September 1917 her father died and the family home was sold. Frederick Gifford had not dis-inherited Grace and she received a legacy of £500, then a considerable amount of money.[1] Her work in 1917 included a design for the cover of *Women in Ancient and Modern Ireland* written by Chrissie Doyle (who had been active in the Daughters of Erin and later in Cumann

Grace's sketch of her husband drawn from memory after his death.

na mBan). Grace also drew a portrait of her husband for a collection of his poetry published after his death, edited by his sister Geraldine.

The year 1917 brought more political activity. Three by-elections were won by Sinn Féin candidates, the first by Grace's father-in-law, Count Plunkett in North Roscommon. Later that year, Joseph Mc-Guinness, then a prisoner in Lewes jail, was elected for South Longford, and Eamon de Valera defeated the Parliamentary Party candidate, Patrick Lynch, KC, in East Clare. Grace helped these campaigns by drawing election posters, work she continued in subsequent years.

When the Sinn Féin Convention met at the Mansion House in Dublin on 19th April that year, Grace was one of four women elected to the executive. The other three were Countess Markievicz, Dr Kathleen Lynn and Kathleen Clarke, the widow of Thomas Clarke who had been executed for his part in the Rising. By temperament and inclination, Grace was not attracted to a public role in politics, but she had become a tragic symbol of 1916 and wanted, in her own way, to work for Irish freedom.

In August 1917, she suffered yet another bereavement when her sister Muriel MacDonagh, was drowned at Skerries, on the north side of Dublin. Muriel was with her two young children, Donagh and Barbara. Although a strong swimmer, she got into difficulty when out of her depth in the water and was unable to save herself. Muriel's death was widely reported in the newspapers. The *Irish Citizen* paid particular tribute to her work in the Irish Women's Franchise League, recalling in particular her portrayal of Queen Maeve in the 'Great Daffodil Fête' held to raise funds in April 1914. Great sympathy was felt for Muriel's family, particularly for her two young children who were now bereft of both their parents. Grace was deeply affected by Muriel's death. It was stated that Grace, not surprisingly, changed a lot after this second bereavement.[2]

The three by-election successes had given a great boost to Sinn Féin. The newly elected members refused to take their seats at Westminster. They had changed the old Sinn Féin policy of seeking dual monarchy with Britain. Meeting in convention in October, a new republican constitution was adopted. It formally expressed:

> Sinn Féin aims at securing the international recognition of Ireland as an Independent Republic. Having achieved that status

the Irish people may by referendum freely choose their own form
of government.[3]

Recognising the changes that had taken place, Arthur Griffith decided
not to go forward as president. With good grace, he supported Eamon
de Valera who was unanimously chosen for the office. By this time, the
secret Irish Republican Brotherhood was planning to reactivate the
Irish Volunteers for the war of independence that was to follow. Sinn
Féin became the political wing of the entire revolutionary movement.

In the spring of 1918, the British government, still grappling with
the war in Europe and increasingly short of manpower, decided to
impose conscription in Ireland. This was a grave mistake and caused
an immediate storm of protest. Members of the Home Rule Party
immediately withdrew from the House of Commons. The Catholic
bishops condemned the proposal in strong terms. A conference was
called by the Lord Mayor of Dublin, Laurence O'Neill. Both Arthur
Griffith and Eamon de Valera attended as delegates for Sinn Féin. It
was decided to call a one-day strike on 23rd April, a move which
effectively showed, except in Belfast, the depth of public feeling on the
issue. As a result, conscription was not extended to Ireland.

Following that defeat, the British government, took a further step
to break the growing power of the separatist movement in Ireland. A
fictitious 'German plot' was concocted by which republicans were said
to be in league with Germany. This was an excuse for a great number
of arrests of so-called 'subversives'. As leaders of Sinn Féin, both Griffith
and de Valera were deported and lodged respectively in Gloucester and
Lincoln jails. A number of women were also arrested. Maud Gonne
MacBride, Countess Markievicz and Kathleen Clarke were lodged in
the women's prison at Holloway, where they were joined by Hanna
Sheehy Skeffington. Hanna had been arrested on her return from the
United States of America. While there, she had been lecturing on
the events of 1916 and the aspirations to political independence of the
Irish people. She managed to see President Wilson and tried to persuade
him to include Ireland among the small nations for whose freedom the
USA was fighting in the war.

These new arrests and imprisonments further alienated public
opinion in Ireland. After the First World War ended in November
1918, a general election was called for December. Sinn Féin made

strenuous efforts to consolidate its place in Irish politics. These efforts were not in vain. The election result was a sweeping victory for Sinn Féin who won seventy-three of the 105 Irish seats, while the old Parliamentary Party retained only six seats. The 1918 election was the first in which women were given the vote and the right to be candidates for election. Their success crowned the efforts of the Irish Women's Franchise League and earlier groups that had fought hard to obtain the vote. Grace, together with her sisters Sydney, Muriel and Nellie, played her own part in that campaign. While her name is not recorded, it is very likely that Grace took part in the women's 'Victory Procession' which escorted Anna Haslam, the great Quaker pioneer for the cause, then almost ninety years old, to record her vote in William Street Courthouse (now the Civic Museum) in central Dublin. Others taking part included Hanna Sheehy Skeffington and Sarah Cecilia Harrison, the artist who was the first woman elected to Dublin Corporation.[4] Countess Markievicz was elected as the first woman member of parliament despite her absence in Holloway. All Sinn Féin members refused to take their seats in Westminster and, with haste, made arrangements to convene the first meeting of Dáil Éireann. It took place on 21st January, 1919 in the Mansion House in Dublin.

Later that year, Grace published seventeen of her cartoons in book form. *To Hold as Twere*, published by Dun Dealgan Press, was dedicated 'To a Beloved Memory'. All depicted were political figures, shown in the distinctive style Grace had adopted. Her wit spared neither friend nor foe. Thus, Sir Edward Carson is portrayed as 'about to rebel', manicuring his nails while a valet brushes his formal clothes. Eamon de Valera is shown as a tight-rope walker, his clothes covered in shamrocks while he carries a flag for the 'Irish Republic' to the League of Nations. Tim Healy appears seated at a table, about to devour a timid witness on toast. Perhaps one of the best cartoons in the collection shows Robert Barton, Minister for Agriculture, as seen by town-dwellers, sitting on a chair while pedicuring the toes of a pig! Sir Horace Plunkett is depicted on his knees, offering a present of 'Dominion Home Rule' to Cathleen Ní Houlihan. A baby marked 'Sinn Féin' lies in her arms as she tells Plunkett she recognises his kind intentions but cannot accept his offer while the child is in her arms. Other subjects include John McCormack, Darrell Figgis and Sir William Orpen.

This collection was widely reviewed and warmly praised. The *Irish Times* noted Grace's skill as a cartoonist and her ability to show her subjects with 'whimsical exaggeration'. The *Evening Herald* found the drawings both clever and entertaining. More detailed reviews were published in other papers such as *Old Ireland*, *The Catholic Bulletin* and *Irish Life*. Compared to an earlier popular cartoonist, 'Dicky' Doyle, Grace's drawings were considered to show greater strength and daring. Her style was very much her own, uninfluenced by the work of others. Special praise was given to two of the sketches – George Moore standing on a pedestal of his own books with a torch held aloft in support of 'Liberty (of Speech)' and the saintly Edward Martyn shown in a state of terror before an apparition of a frivolous Parisienne. This collection brought a much needed tonic of laughter to a war-weary Ireland that Christmas.

The Volunteers had reorganised themselves as the Irish Republican Army to continue the struggle for freedom. Unlike the men of 1916, they did not seize important buildings and try to hold them. A guerrilla army operated in flying columns, carrying out raids and ambushes on the British military forces. Dáil Éireann had been banned as illegal and could only operate underground. It met from time to time but had no control over the actions of the IRA. As 1920 unfolded the War of Independence was in full swing. The Royal Irish Constabulary was unable to cope. The British Government raised men in England, mainly unemployed ex-soldiers and ex-officers, to fight in Ireland. The 'Black-and-Tans' (so-called because of their khaki and black uniforms) and the 'Auxiliaries' (as the ex-officers were called) tried to break the IRA. Methods used caused public concern in Britain, where Lloyd George's coalition government was attacked constantly in both parliament and the newspapers.

Finally, a truce was arranged in July 1921, and later that year negotiations began with the British government. Leading the Irish delegation was Grace's old friend Arthur Griffith. Hopes were high that a settlement would be achieved. After a tortuous process, the Treaty was signed on 6th December of that year. The Treaty brought greater tragedy to Ireland, as the country quickly divided into pro-Treaty and anti-Treaty factions. Grace and her sisters had greatly admired the political leadership of Griffith. However, his action in signing the Treaty agreement alienated them totally. Like most of the

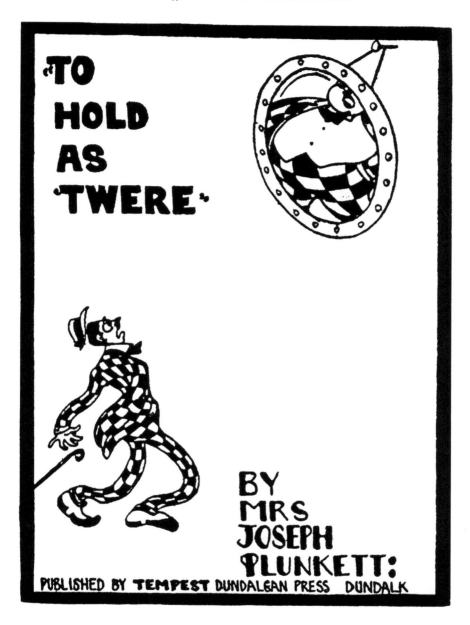

The cover of *To Hold As 'Twere*, a book of cartoons by Mrs Joseph Plunkett, published by Dundalgan Press, Dundalk, 1919.

Edward Carson, Dublin-born lawyer who led the Ulster Opposition to Home Rule.

Eamon de Valera, revolutionary, politican, and later President of Ireland

Timothy Healy, famous barrister and member for Wexford of the Irish parliamentary party in the House of Commons. He later became first Governor-General of the Irish Free State.

Robert Barton, Wicklow-born politician who became Minister for Agriculture in the first Dáil Éireann.

Horace Plunkett, leader of the movement to promote co-operation in farming, became a Senator of the Irish Free State after independence.

Darrell Figgis, writer of poetry novels and plays. He worked as a journalist and became Honorary Secretary of Sinn Fein from 1917–1919. Elected to the Dail for County Dublin in 1922. He died in 1925.

John McCormack, famous Irish-born operatic and concert tenor.

William Orpen, the artist and portrait painter. He taught art in London and in the School of Art in Dublin where Grace Gifford was one of his pupils.

George Moore, the novelist, returned to Dublin from London in 1901. He participated in the Irish Literary Revival and the founding of the Abbey Theatre.

widows and relatives of the 1916 leaders, Grace saw the Treaty as a total betrayal of the proclaimed Republic for which her husband and his companions-in-arms had died.

Passions rose at an alarming rate on both sides though neither supporters nor opponents of the Treaty expected civil war. A permanent 'split', more bitter than that which had followed Parnell's divorce case thirty years earlier, was on the way. Throughout the years of struggle there was no time to consider what form of settlement, short of an independent republic, would be acceptable to Irish men and women. All efforts had been of necessity concentrated on political and military campaigns. Added to this tragedy was the fact that both sides in this bitter confrontation loved their country equally and held its welfare at heart.

NOTES

1. I am grateful to Maeve Donnelly, Grace's niece, for this information.
2. See entry for Grace in Theo Snoddy's *Dictionary of Irish Artists* (Wolfhound Press, 1996). A letter to the author from Geraldine Dillon in 1982 states Grace changed a lot after Muriel's death, becoming a 'loner and often very difficult'.
3. See Dorothy Macardle's *The Irish Republic* Appendix 4.
4. See report in the *Freeman's Journal* on 16th December.

CHAPTER SEVEN

Civil War

THE TREATY was ratified by the Dáil on 7th January, 1922 after weeks of agonising debate. The majority in favour was small. Sixty-four members supported it and fifty-seven opposed it. The army quickly divided into pro-Treaty and anti-Treaty factions. This was an ominous development as armies are always powerful in post-revolutionary periods. Opponents of the Treaty had three main objections. Firstly, it did not bring about the full independence aspired to by those who fought for freedom. Secondly, its insistence that all members of the Dáil take an oath of allegiance to the British sovereign. This became an emotive issue as many members felt unable to give such a pledge of loyalty. Thirdly, many feared that the Treaty would result in permanent partition of the country which had been imposed in 1920 by the Government of Ireland Act. However, many people cherished the hope that the Boundary Commission would change the position of the six counties in Northern Ireland. The imperial trappings of a Governor-General appointed by Britain went against the grain with many Dáil deputies, as it did with the general populace.

After the Dáil vote was taken, Eamon de Valera resigned as President and was replaced by Arthur Griffith. A provisional government was formed to hold power until the next general election. This was a very uneasy and complex period. This continued until the final crisis which precipitated the so-called and bitter 'war of brothers'. This happened in June, following a general election resulting in a majority in favour of the Treaty settlement. Sir Henry Wilson, a high-ranking British Army officer and MP for North Down, was assassinated on his own doorstep in London. Wilson had been a bitter opponent of Ireland's claim to independence. As military adviser to the Northern government, he had urged coercion against opponents of the Treaty. His killing was apparently carried out under an old Republican directive that had never been revoked.

This violent act led to grave problems in Ireland. In Dublin, a group of republicans led by Rory O'Connor seized and occupied the Four Courts in defiance of the government. Other buildings in O'Connell Street were also seized by republicans, led by Cathal Brugha and others. Brugha had fought bravely in 1916 and later in the War of Independence. As member for Waterford, he presided at the first meeting of Dáil Éireann on 21st January, 1919 and became Minister for Defence, a post he held until January 1922. A bitter opponent of the Treaty, he castigated his former comrades-in-arms who accepted it, using most intemperate language.

The British government now put severe pressure on Michael Collins and the provisional government to come to grips with the republicans who had defied it in this way. As chairman of the provisional government, he was virtually ordered to use force to end the occupations. On 28th June, Collins yielded to these demands. His order to the forces to evacuate the Four Courts was disregarded. Artillery bombardment began. Two days later, the garrison surrendered. Within a week other occupied buildings were blasted and burned. Cathal Brugha was mortally wounded as he emerged, gun in hand, from a burning building. He died two days later, on 7th July, in the Mater hospital where attempts to save him failed.

In the previous March, Grace had written to *The Republic* to explain her opposition to the Treaty. She viewed the republic proclaimed in 1916 as a reality which should not be abandoned. She wrote similar letters to the *Irish Independent*. At the same time she appealed to people to remember that both Arthur Griffith and Eamon de Valera were patriots. She expressed the hope that there would be no recriminations against them. She thus showed a generous spirit at a time of widespread bitterness. However, some months later Grace's views seem to have hardened. The writer R. M. Fox later stated that he saw her on the roof of the Four Courts in June, blowing a bugle to summon support for the republicans.[1] She attended the funeral of Cathal Brugha in July and joined in handing out a type-written notice to old comrades who had become Treaty supporters.[2] In the name of Cathal Brugha's widow they were asked to step out of the ranks of mourners. This caused great hurt as those rejected did as they had been asked and left the scene.

In a letter to the *Irish Independent* Grace raised the issue of votes for women. In her view there was no need for the Irish Women's Franchise

League to continue its campaign as full rights as citizens had been given to women in the 1916 Proclamation. Though legally she may not have been correct, the new constitution of the Irish Free State put the matter beyond doubt. Full voting rights were given to women over the age of twenty-one.[3]

As events of the Civil War unfolded, repressive measures against republicans increased. Arthur Griffith, worn out by his years of toil, and bitterly disappointed that the Treaty had not brought peace to his country, died suddenly in Dublin on 12th August. His death, at the comparatively early age of fifty-one, shocked the Irish people. Only ten days later Michael Collins was killed in an ambush at Beal na Blath in his native Cork. Collins, who had become Commander-in-Chief of the Free State Army when the Civil War began, was only thirty-two years old. His stature was such that many who opposed his politics were shocked and saddened. The awful reality of civil war was brought home in all its harshness.

The new head of government was William T. Cosgrave. He faced a difficult task trying to grapple with a chaotic situation. The political efforts of Eamon de Valera and others to bring an end to the fighting did not succeed. As a result, military leaders took over and the politicians were disregarded. Executions of republicans began following summary trials by special courts set up in haste. Worse was to follow before the end of 1922. On 24th November, Erskine Childers, member of the Dáil for Wicklow, who had taken the anti-Treaty side in the Civil War, was executed before a Habeas Corpus application on his behalf could be heard by the courts. He had been arrested at Glendalough House in Laragh, the home of his mother's family (the Bartons), and charged with having a revolver in his possession. The small pistol had been a gift from Michael Collins. Following the shooting dead, on 7th December, of Sean Hales, a Dáil deputy who had supported the Treaty, the government decided drastic action was necessary to protect the lives of elected representatives. On 8th December, four republican prisoners in Mountjoy jail were taken out and shot without trial. Rory O'Connor, Liam Mellowes, Joseph McKelvey and Richard Barrett paid the supreme penalty for a crime with which they had no connection. Even Free State supporters were appalled and uneasy at such draconian action.

Throughout the Civil War, vast numbers of republicans were

arrested and incarcerated in jails all over the country without trial or charge. Women and men suffered the same fate. Grace was arrested with many others on 6th February, 1923 and detained in Kilmainham jail for about three months.[4] Others held there included Dorothy Macardle, Nora Connolly O'Brien, Mary McSwiney, Dr Kathleen Lynn and Nell Ryan. Maud Gonne MacBride, first held in Mountjoy jail, was in Kilmainham jail from 10th April until her release later that month. At the time of Grace's arrest, a large number of women prisoners were transferred from Mountjoy to Kilmainham. Some had been in Kilmainham in 1916 and were familiar with the conditions there. For those who saw it for the first time in 1923, it was a grim and gloomy sight. The cells were small and sparsely furnished with a table, a stool and a mattress on the floor. Some were lit by gaslight but others by a candle. Meals were brought by convicted prisoners at fixed times. The food was cooked by women convicts brought from Mountjoy for that purpose. The political status of the women interned was recognised to an extent. They could move around outside their cells and talk to one another. Food parcels were sent in to them and those who could afford it could order from a local shop. They could also write and receive letters.

Grace occupied herself as best she could during her detention. She painted on the walls of her cell, most notably a Madonna and Child which became famous as the *Kilmainham Madonna*.[5] Flowers were kept there and women prisoners formed the habit of dropping in to say their prayers. Such quiet moments were very welcome in the overcrowded conditions of the jail. Many of the women found the place oppressive with its grim memories of suffering and death. In addition, some of them were handled very roughly by the raw recruits in the Free State Army. There was a large presence from Cumann na mBan, some of them highly educated women, and they tried to help in various ways. Classes were organised to cater for the women in accordance with their educational standards. The basic 'Three Rs' were taught where required. Dancing lessons were given by Mrs Lavery. Irish language and culture were promoted strongly and Dorothy Macardle gave Irish history lessons three times a week.

Some of the women found a way of cooking food in their cells using a gas jet in an opening behind the cell door. By placing a stool on top of the small table, water could be heated to make tea. Food could be cooked holding an enamel plate. These activities must have created a fire hazard but fortunately there were no fires. The Dublin prisoners also managed to talk to relatives and friends who came to the outside of the jail. They could shout from the windows of the third floor. This custom was depicted in a painting by Jack B. Yeats dated 1923.

On the seventh anniversary of Easter 1916, the women prisoners in Kilmainham organised their own commemoration. As widow of one of the executed leaders, Grace took a prominent part in the ceremonial, as did Nora Connolly, the daughter of James. Early in the afternoon all the women marched into the bleak execution yard. Grace unfurled the tricolour flag, laid a laurel wreath and spoke about her husband. Lily O'Brennan, sister-in-law of Eamonn Ceannt, paid her tribute and recalled her own memories of the Rising. Ellen Humphries, the sister of The O'Rahilly who had been killed near the General Post Office before the surrender, led the traditional Catholic prayer, the Rosary, speaking in Irish. That evening a concert was given on the ground floor of the East wing. Joseph Mary Plunkett's poem 'Treason' was recited and one of Patrick Pearse's plays, *The Singer*, was performed. The concert ended with the *Soldier's Song*, composed by Peadar Kearney and Patrick Heeney in 1907, which later became the National Anthem of the new state.[6]

During her stay in Kilmainham, Grace wrote a short biographical sketch of her husband. Dated 3rd May, it was handwritten on a double sheet of foolscap paper. Grace praised the 'noble character' of Plunkett and recalled his dreams of what a free Ireland could achieve. His practical skills and knowledge of weaponry ensured that the Rising would have 'proper appliances'. She quoted with approval a tribute to her husband by Peter McBrien which described his personality as 'a rare mixture of vivacity and repose'. For Grace, his conversation was always full of lightning wit.

Grace was released some time in May after the Civil War came to its uneasy end following the order of Frank Aiken[7] to end the fighting and dump arms. A bitter division in Irish political life had been created. It endured for many years and is still present to some extent. In 1922–23 the Free State government saw its opponents as fanatics whose resistance tried to sabotage its efforts to bring peace and order to the country. Republicans felt a lasting bitterness as they faced military defeat. Seventy-nine of them had been executed. Grace

Painted on wall in Kilmainham Jail by Mrs. Joseph Plunkett.

The Madonna and Child, painted by Grace Plunkett during her imprisonment in Kilmainham Jail in 1923.

herself felt a deep hostility to the new state which, in her view, had betrayed the cause for which her husband had given his life.

NOTES

1. See R. M. Fox *Rebel Irishwomen* (Talbot Press, 1935) pp.75–89.
2. See letter of Jennie Wyse Power to her daughter Nancy on 11 July, 1922. The letter is among the Mulcahy papers in the archives of University College, Dublin.
3. This extension was not granted in Britain and Northern Ireland until 1928.
4. The army records do not contain the date of her release.
5. The painting, which had faded badly over the years, has now been restored as part of the refurbishment of the jail.
6. Dorothy Macardle wrote an article on the commemoration which was published in the paper *Éire* on 12th May, 1923.
7. Chief-of-Staff of the Republican army.

CHAPTER EIGHT

The Aftermath

AFTER the Civil War ended, the Free State government had control of the country and settled down to the task of creating stability and firm administration. Grace's position was extremely difficult. She had no home of her own and very little money. Bitterness against republicans was so strong that she could expect no material help from the government, despite her status as the widow of one of the 1916 leaders. Her talent as an artist was her only real asset. She also had the friendship and sympathy of her fellow republicans – that great camaraderie that endures among those who have fought for the same cause.

Grace also benefited from the practical help of her sisters Katie and Nellie. It was in Katie's home on the north side of Dublin that she stayed for some time after her release from Kilmainham.[1] Sydney Czira, who had returned from the USA in 1921, was also there for a while with her young son, Finian. Grace had a very close and loving relationship with her third sister, Nellie Donnelly, who had separated from her husband and had a daughter, Maeve, to rear on her own. That child became a strong focus of interest for Grace. She also was concerned for the welfare of Muriel's two children, Donagh and Barbara, for whose upbringing and education a trust fund had been established. All of Grace's brothers, except the actor Blake Gifford, had left Ireland as young adults. Some of them continued to write letters to Katie and Nellie but otherwise there was little contact. Grace had a strong common interest with Blake, who acted in the Gate Theatre, and often travelled abroad to take part in its productions.

It appears that Grace did not always get on well with her sister Sydney. Using the name John Brennan as her pseudonym, Sydney established her own career as a writer and broadcaster. Often described as a fierce and colourful personality, Sydney was more intellectual than Grace. Some sources suggest she regarded Grace as something of a lightweight.

75

Grace resumed her work. It was very difficult to earn her living as fees were small and commissions hard to obtain. Post-Civil War Ireland was not a good place for artists. The economy was depressed and remained so for a long time. Grace was anxious to have her own home in the city as soon as possible. Subsequently, she was reported to be living in poverty in a small apartment in Westmoreland Street above some offices. One story relates that she spent a bleak Christmas on her own there, with little food and her only companion a mouse which had come out of its hole.[2] Grace later moved to a better apartment at 15, Parnell Square where she remained for a long time. She liked to live in or near the city centre where she could follow her tastes for theatres, art galleries and exhibitions. It was also more convenient for the newspaper and magazine editors who purchased her work. In addition, Grace had a wide circle of friends in the city and she liked to see them regularly. At the same time, she was something of a 'loner' who liked her own space. She needed a certain amount of solitude. By her own nature, and because of her upbringing in a house full of servants, Grace was not domesticated. She disliked catering and cooking for herself. She formed the habit of eating lunch in restaurants in the city, notably those attached to the Carlton and Savoy cinemas in O'Connell Street. There she often met famous actors of the period such as Michael MacLiammoir, Hilton Edwards and Jimmy O'Dea. Grace frequently did the posters for the latter's Christmas pantomimes. These annual entertainments were a regular treat for children. They were performed in the Gaiety theatre, where the tradition still continues.

Grace did a lot of commercial work in the 1920s and later. She drew cartoons for products such as Dromona Soap, Fitzpatrick's shoes and the goods produced by the newly formed Gaeltacht industries. Periodicals such as *Irish Life, Dublin Opinion, Irish Fun* and the *Irish Tatler and Sketch* regularly published these sketches, as did the *Sunday Independent*. One of the cartoons which Grace did to advertise Jacob's biscuits was accompanied by a rhyme:

> There was a young man from Fingal[3]
> Who went to a fancy dress ball
> Said he 'I will risk it
> And go as a biscuit',
> A dog ate him up in the hall!

Another of Grace's cartoons, to advertise the Irish Sweepstakes which had been recently established, depicts a large fat bride with a small thin husband. The caption underneath was as follows: 'Look at the risk some people run. You only risk ten shillings to win a fortune!'[4]

Grace's cartoons in the 1920s often related to political events and well-known personalities. In 1925 *Irish Fun* published a sketch of a man and woman sitting by a fire. The woman asks: 'Isn't it a pity Gilbert and Sullivan[5] didn't visit Dublin this year?' The man replies: 'Suppose they thought the Ulster Parliament opened by a Catholic Viceroy was Gilbertian enough.' This referred to the formal opening of the Stormont parliament for the six Northern Counties, an occasion best remembered for the moving speech of King George V in which he expressed the hope that Irish people of all traditions would try to build a better future for their country.

Grace signed her work in various ways. Sometimes she identified herself as 'Mrs Joseph Plunkett' and this form was used in a certificate she designed for the Leinster School of Music in August 1926. Sometimes she signed as 'Grace Vandeleur Plunkett'. Arthur Vandeleur was Grace's grand-uncle on her mother's side. He had established a co-operative colony at Ralahine in County Clare in the nineteenth century. Grace was proud of this relationship. Likewise, she was proud of another grand-uncle, the artist Frederick William Burton, although she never used his name. As time passed and her work became better known, she signed simply as 'Grace Plunkett'.

An early admirer of Grace's art was Joseph Holloway, the Dublin architect who became famous as a regular theatre-goer. He kept a detailed journal of the various performances he attended, notably first nights. Holloway accumulated a vast collection of material relating to the Abbey and other theatres in the Dublin of his day. He often helped Grace by purchasing her work and she confided in him about her problems in making a living. In 1913, Holloway lent six of her sketches for an exhibition of Irish art in Whitechapel, London.[6]

Sometime after 1916, Grace met a Dublin solicitor, John Burke, who became a lifelong friend. After his marriage in 1924 to Mary Ellen Jordan from Lurgan in County Armagh, Grace became a frequent visitor to their home in Rathgar. His wife had adopted the Irish form of her name, Máire, which she pronounced 'Maurey' and she welcomed

Grace warmly into their family circle. The couple had one child, a daughter Ann, who remembers Grace very well.

John Burke was deeply interested in art and became one of the directors of the National Gallery. He often bought Grace's sketches and encouraged her in various ways. As her legal adviser he tried to make Grace more practical and businesslike in marketing her work. At times she was generous to a fault in presenting sketches to her friends. She also tended to be overgenerous with money, leaving herself short on occasion. In addition, John Burke acted as a spiritual guide to Grace. He was a devout Catholic, and she, like most converts, was very serious about her adopted faith. Despite this, Grace, with her impish sense of humour, could not resist poking some gentle fun at her mentor. In a cartoon of 'John Burke, Saint and Solicitor' done in 1928, she depicted her friend dragging a doctor's patient to a chapel, despite the doctor's warning that the invalid had typhoid! Likewise, Grace inscribed a book, *Lyra Celtica*, which she gave as a Christmas gift in 1932 'to my spiritual director John Burke (already canonised by acclamation)!'

Among fellow republicans who kept in touch with Grace was Eamon de Valera. Later in her life Grace recalled a conversation they had some time in 1926. De Valera was then very despondent about the future, seeing no way forward for those who had opposed the Treaty. He confided his fears, ending with the question: 'Oh, Gracie, Gracie, what am I going to do?'[7] Within a short time, de Valera found a political path when his new republican party, Fianna Fáil, was founded.

As an attractive, stylish and amusing woman, Grace had many admirers. Some of them may have hoped to marry her. While she enjoyed male company, Grace does not seem to have taken any of those admirers seriously. Close as she was to her sister Nellie, Grace never discussed with her any romantic interest she might have felt.[8] On the whole it appears she had no wish to remarry. She was intensely proud of her position as the widow of her heroic husband and remained so for the rest of her life. Perhaps she had also become accustomed to an independent life where she was free to concentrate on her art and follow the various interests she had developed over the years. At the end of 1929, Grace's cartoons became more widely known when a selection was published in book form. Colm O'Lochlainn, who had worked closely with Joseph Plunkett in the preparations for the

1916 Rising, was a great admirer of Grace's art. His publishing firm, 'At the Sign of the Three Candles' in Fleet Street, Dublin, took the initiative in bringing out *Twelve Nights at the Abbey Theatre*. Lady Gregory wrote the introduction, praising warmly Grace's talent as a humorist. She recalled a song she had written for the central character in one of her own plays *The Jester*.

> And so I follow after
> Lycurgus who was wise
> To the little god of laughter
> I pay my sacrifice.

Remembering the laughter the Abbey Players had brought with their fine work on the stage, she thought they would not object to 'pay their sacrifice' in the portraits drawn. Although the book was a limited edition for not more than two hundred subscribers, it was reviewed in several papers and periodicals. The playwright T. C. Murray wrote that Grace had restored to Dublin the note of gaiety which had been characteristic of the city. He praised the 'whimsical mockery' of the artist and the beautiful craft of the publication. Writing in the *Irish Times* Caulfield Orpen noted the fine sense of design in the groups of actors depicted. By this time Grace's style as an artist had developed more fully. There was no sign of the unevenness of her earlier work.

Those who subscribed to the publication were very pleased with the result. Many others were disappointed when they could not obtain copies. A second edition was suggested and Grace was approached about it. She decided she would prefer to have a second set of her cartoons published. This came out in October 1930 with the title *Doctors Recommend It: An Abbey Tonic in Twelve Doses*. Again it was a limited edition but this time there were five hundred subscribers. The introduction was written by T. C. Murray, whose fine play *Autumn Fire* was the subject of one of the cartoons. He praised Grace's 'impish fancy' and her talent which he considered supreme in its own line. He thought the collection would be welcomed by everyone who cherished 'the wisdom of laughter'. Reviews of this second collection were very enthusiastic. Both Dublin evening papers, the *Herald* and the *Mail*, praised the brilliance of the artist, recalling also the early personal tragedy Grace had suffered – an experience which could have broken many women. Other reviews noted her pre-eminence as a black-and-white artist and master of kindly caricature. From this time on, Grace was firmly established in her chosen work and she had her niche in the cultural life of Dublin.

Examples of Grace's commercial work in the 1920–1930 period.

GRACE PLUNKETT

Talking of Cuts . . .

Did you ever get a suit cut by Gaeltacht
Industries Ltd.? It's the one cut nobody
ever finds fault with. There you'll find the
widest selection of hand-woven tweeds and
worsteds from the leading Irish mills. And
the prices are surprisingly moderate.

Gaeltacht Industries, Ltd.

39 Nassau Street, Dublin

OK-B

GRACE PLUNKETT.

Look at the risk some people run. You only risk 10/- to win a fortune.
Buy your Derby Sweepstake Ticket now. Receiving Offices at the

GRACE PLUNKETT

SHE—"Isn't it a pity the Gilbert and Sullivan Operas didn't visit Dublin this year ?"

HE—"Suppose they thought the Ulster Parliament opened by a Catholic Viceroy was Gilbertian enough ! "

Grace Plunkett's view of the opening of the Northern Ireland Parliament in 1925.

John Burke was Grace Plunkett's friend, legal and spiritual adviser.

TWELVE NIGHTS *at the* ABBEY THEATRE

A BOOK OF DRAWINGS BY GRACE PLUNKETT

Printed for the Subscribers by Colm O Lochlainn
at the sign of the Three Candles in Fleet Street Dublin
1929

The cover of *Twelve Nights at the Abbey Theatre,* by Grace Plunkett, published
by the Three Candles, Dublin, 1929.

'Juno and the Paycock' by Sean O'Casey. The players are Sara Allgood,
F.J. McCormick and Barry Fitzgerald.

'The Far-off Hills' by Lennox Robinson. The players are P.J. Carolan, Eileen Crowe, F.J. McCormick, Maureen Delany, Arthur Shields and Shelah Richards.

'The Well of the Saints' by John Millington Synge. The players are Peter Nolan, Michael J. Dolan, Sara Allgood and F.J. McCormick.

'The Plough and the stars' by Sean O'Casey. The players are Maureen Delany, Eric Gorman, Michael J. Dolan, P.J. Carolan and T. Moran.

'An Imaginary Conversation' by Conal O'Riordan. The players are Arthur Shields, Eileen Crowe, and Barry Fitzgerald.

'The Playboy of the Western World' by John Millington Synge. The players are Michael Scott, Maureen Delaney, F.J. McCormick, Arthur Shields, P.J. Carolan, Barry Fitzgerald, and Eileen Crowe.

NOTES

1. The exact address was 7, Bushfield Park, Philipsburgh Avenue, Fairview. Katie had lost her husband, Walter Harris Wilson, in the 1918 influenza epidemic.
2. This report is contained in the reminiscences of Cathal Gannon, a later friend of Grace. I am grateful to him and his son Charles for allowing me to see the document.
3. Fingal is a district on the north side of Dublin. It is possible that Grace wrote the rhyme.
4. Ten shillings then was worth a great deal. Many people worked for salaries of a few hundred pounds per annum.
5. The Gilbert and Sullivan comic operas were regularly performed in Dublin by the visiting D'Oyly Carte company from London. Later the local Rathmines and Rathgar Musical Society carried on the tradition.
6. Many of Grace's cartoons are preserved in the Holloway collections in the National Library of Ireland. Two books about Holloway have been published in the USA, both edited by Robert Hogan and Michael J. O'Neill. They appeared in 1967 and 1969.
7. I am grateful to Professor Kevin B. Nowlan for this story. He remembers Grace telling him of the conversation in the year 1940.
8. Information given in an interview by Maeve Donnelly.

CHAPTER NINE

The Middle Years

THE 1930s and 1940s were productive and active periods in Grace's life. Her material circumstances improved following the coming to power of Eamon de Valera and his Fianna Fáil party in 1932. Within a short time Grace received a Civil List pension which meant that she was no longer totally dependent on her earnings as an artist. Indeed, her old friend Joseph Holloway is said to have cursed the day she received her pension, fearing that she might never draw again! This proved to be mistaken and Grace continued to do the commercial and theatrical cartoons for which she was well known. She celebrated her pension with a party for her friends in the famous Jammet's restaurant, buying sweets lavishly afterwards for the children of one of her guests.[1] This new financial security was a great benefit to Grace and she was lastingly grateful to Eamon de Valera who had arranged it. She could now afford a more comfortable lifestyle which included travelling abroad. She often went to Paris, a city she had loved all her life, where she could visit the various museums and art galleries in which she delighted.

During this period Grace lived for a long time at 11, Nassau Street where she rented the top flat in the house. This centre city location was very convenient. Her apartment had a balcony overlooking the grounds of Trinity College. There she would sit with her friends on fine sunny evenings, watching the students playing cricket and rugby. A new interest was her membership of the Old Dublin Society which she joined shortly after its foundation in 1934. The society promoted the study of the history and antiquities of the city. Papers were read at weekly meetings in the winter months and, during the summer, visits were arranged to interesting places. The first president of the Society was Alderman Tom Kelly whom Grace would have known quite well as he had been a strong Sinn Féin supporter in his earlier days. Among the other members were the distinguished feminist Hanna Sheehy Skeffington and also Professor Mary Hayden who taught history in

University College. Grace's sisters Nellie and Sydney also joined the Society, as did the Misses Lil and Eva McNamara who were old friends. (Their aunt, Mary Perolz, of Huguenot origin, was a well-known member of Cumann na mBan who had been involved in the 1916 Rising.) The Old Dublin Society held its meetings at the City Assembly House in South William Street. This was a very short walk from Grace's flat and she often brought her friends back there after the meetings.[2]

As time passed Grace's contact with the Plunkett family diminished. Her claim to a share in the wealth of the family had been greatly resented, especially by her mother-in-law, Josephine, who apparently regarded the eleventh hour marriage to her son as opportunistic on Grace's part. The Countess was tough and mean in money matters – a fact that has been admitted by members of her own family. In the memoirs of her daughter, Geraldine, the justice of Grace's claim was conceded. The Countess was unreasonable and remained so. She ignored the wishes of her son, that his share in the family property should go to Grace. Despite the fact that Grace lived in poverty until receiving her Civil List pension in 1932, a fact apparently well-known to her in-laws, the Countess refused to make any financial provision for her. Eventually Grace felt she had no option but to take legal action to enforce her rights.

The will made by Joseph on Easter Sunday 1916, in which he left everything to Grace, was invalid for two reasons. Firstly, it had only one witness while the law requires two. Secondly, the fact that the marriage to Grace took place after the will was made, automatically revoked it. While it might have been possible to get over the first difficulty, by regarding the will as that of a soldier, the second problem could not be overcome.

In December 1934, Grace issued legal proceedings against Count Plunkett and his wife. As his widow, she claimed her late husband's share in the estate of his predeceased uncle, J. J. Cranny. The Count and Countess were executors and trustees of his will. The action seems to have come as a shock to the Plunkett family. They had not expected it and found the attendant newspaper reports embarrassing. In the circumstances, it was decided to settle the case before it could be heard in full by the court. Grace received £700 plus her legal costs. The formal consent was approved by the court on 30th March, 1935.[3] The fact that Grace had taken the matter to court was resented, rightly or wrongly, by her in-laws and alienated them even further.[4]

Grace's straitened financial position from 1916 until 1932 had been well known to her fellow republican Hanna Sheehy Skeffington. Hanna tried to obtain practical help for Grace from republican sympathisers in the United States.[5]

It has to be admitted that Grace was not always an easy person to get along with – she was reserved and could be prickly at times. Even her friends considered her behaviour a bit unpredictable. However, those who knew her best enjoyed her lively company and made allowances for her mercurial temperament, much of which they felt was due to the tragedies she had suffered in her youth. The memories of these events haunted Grace for the rest of her life.

Grace's friends in the Old Dublin Society included a talented young man, Cathal Gannon, whom she had first met at the home of the McNamara sisters. Cathal worked in Guinness's brewery. Despite little formal education he developed a strong interest in cultural matters and wrote two papers for the Society in its early years. Cathal often joined the groups of friends who visited Grace in her flat. Indeed he became very useful to her as a handyman who did odd jobs. He remembers driving Grace and his brother (in his father's car) to an all-night party given in 1936 by Ned Sheehy and his artist wife, Anna Kelly. The couple had a cottage in the lovely Glencree Valley in the Dublin mountains and the party was held there. The cottage was beautifully whitewashed inside with a wide border on the floor. A gramophone played Debussy while a young girl performed classical ballet in her bare feet. As her contribution to the food Grace had brought a parcel of kippers which were cooked and eaten. The party lasted until dawn broke over Lough Bray, a wonderful sight.[6]

Grace was fond of sewing and made some of her own clothes. She reserved her free time on Sundays for this activity and did not like to be interrupted by friends calling. Grace enjoyed the summer visits of the Old Dublin Society to interesting places. On these occasions her mischievous sense of fun often surfaced. While being shown around Christ Church Cathedral in Dublin (a Church of Ireland establishment), Grace decided to act the strong Protestant. Pointing to the candles on the altar of the Lady Chapel she asked if they were not 'Popish' trappings. The guide responded, no doubt with some surprise, that the candles were not lit, unlike those in Catholic churches. On another occasion, while visiting the Catholic church in Drogheda where the head of the martyred Archbishop Oliver Plunkett was displayed, Grace noticed a nearby painting of Christ coming out of Pilate's house with no sign of having been beaten. With some irreverence she asked: 'Doesn't he look as if he was coming out of Max Factor?' A nearby priest could not resist laughing at the jest.

Ann Burke remembers the wedding gift Grace gave to Mollie O'Neill, a young girl who worked as a maid in the Burke home. It was a rubbish bin with a chamber pot inside! During the years of the Second World War Grace continued to be a regular visitor to the Burke home. She usually came for informal meals in the big kitchen. With war-time rationing and shortages these visits were a welcome break for Grace. She always brought some of her own rations of tea and butter with her so as not to deplete the supplies of the family.

During the 1930s and 1940s Grace and her sisters Nellie and Sydney became concerned about the eventual location of the many mementoes they had from the troubled times. In 1935 Grace wrote to the *Irish Press* stating that she was keeping all souvenirs of her husband until a proper museum was provided to house them. One of the items she held was the diary kept by Joseph in Easter week 1916 and another was the 'code message stolen from Dublin Castle' which purported to disclose plans to arrest the leaders. Eventually most of the items were donated to the National Museum and Kilmainham jail. Cathal Gannon remembers that he persuaded Grace to give all her papers (including the love letters from her husband) to the National Library and this was done after her death.

A souvenir of what may have been a romantic involvement of Grace survives in an undated letter with sketch attached. It came from an artist identified as Norman M. who wrote from Hampstead in London.[7] It seems that Grace had known the writer since her student days under Orpen who, in her view, had not recognised the young man's talent. Grace had asked Norman if he could get her some stockings which she had been unable to find in Dublin. His reply was flirtatious as he protested that he should not be asked to buy stockings for her in London when he would be unable to see her wearing them in Dublin! The sketch at the end of the letter shows a 'Mr Self-conscious' at a shop counter. He tries to explain what he wants to an amused assistant in the hearing of a dowager-like customer seated regally in a chair. The letter concludes:

> Well, Grace, this letter must cease. I wish I were beside you so that I could give you all the kisses I now send! I can't count them – I send you so many – and with my arms tight round you and your lips on mine I bid you good-bye for a little while only – I hope.[8]

Grace's nephews and nieces were growing up in the 1930s. In July of 1934, the *Daily Sketch* newspaper reported that she was bringing Donagh MacDonagh, then a law student, for a holiday to Spain. Grace continued to take an interest in his welfare and that of his sister Barbara who later married the well-known actor Liam Redmond. Donagh became a barrister and was appointed as a District Justice in 1941. He was a man of literary talent who developed a career as a writer of poetry, drama and ballads. He also broadcast and edited many publications. Grace was very proud of Donagh's abilities and enjoyed his company. His most successful play was the exuberant *Happy as Larry* which was translated into various European languages.

Grace remained very close to her sister Nellie and visited her constantly. She watched over Nellie's daughter Maeve with affection, seeing her grow into a handsome girl with more than her share of the Gifford good looks. In 1940, Grace wrote a short unfinished verse about Maeve:

> And God took clay
> For in his secret mind he saw your face
> And bent his fingers to the lovely shape
> With curves and eddies of the mountain wind
>
> He formed your hair ...[9]

Maeve fully returned her aunt Grace's affection. Both she and her mother remained in close contact with Grace to the end of her life. Living alone as Grace did, such family relationships were important to her. Likewise she valued her friends and enjoyed their company. Despite her solitary nature, she did not want to be alone all the time.

NOTES

1. For this information I am indebted to Ann Burke whose parents told her about the celebration.
2. Professor Kevin B. Nowlan remembers being there with a group about the year 1940 when he was a young student.
3. The record number of the High Court case is 3,787 for the year 1934. The Court file is available in the National Archives. My thanks are due to Gregory O'Connor who traced the documents and made them available for my inspection.
4. See Theo Snoddy *Dictionary of Irish Artists* (Wolfhound Press, 1996) in which the views of Geraldine Dillon about Grace are quoted. Geraldine thought Grace could have made more money from her art if she had been more businesslike. While this criticism has some truth, it seems Geraldine had little understanding of Grace's difficulty in making a living in the years 1916–32.
5. See *Hanna Sheehy Skeffington* by Margaret Ward (Attic Press, 1997), p.223. Grace had received some help from the National Aid Committee but it was soon exhausted.
6. These memories are recorded in the reminiscences of Cathal Gannon already cited. Cathal later became well-known as a maker of harpsichords.
7. Ann Burke believes the surname was Morrow.
8. Grace later gave the letter and sketch to John Burke who had it framed.
9. Maeve Donnelly showed me the original poem which is framed. Two copies of it are included in Ms. 21,597 in the National Library. Even in later years Maeve's handsome face retained its distinction. She died in December 1997.

CHAPTER TEN

The Final Curtain

T HE LAST YEARS of Grace's life were darkened by the health problems which began to trouble her in the late 1940s. A young student who interviewed Grace for a research project in 1948 found her looking gaunt and frail.[1] In 1950, Ann Burke remembers that she and her mother helped Grace into St Vincent's hospital, then situated in St Stephen's Green – a short distance from Nassau Street where Grace still lived. Grace was then very weak, unable to carry her own light case. Despite this frailty Grace was in good spirits, joking with the elderly nurse who showed her to her bed that she knew she was going to be 'bossed'! Grace had problems with her heart and had been attending her medical adviser, Dr Eamon O'hOgain, for some time.

During her stay in hospital, Kathleen O'Connell, secretary to Eamon de Valera, called to arrange a visit from her 'Chief' who was then leader of the opposition in the Dáil. He came in due course. Grace appreciated his concern but found it difficult to talk to her guest. It seems she had always been a little in awe of him, as indeed many people were. When de Valera told her he spent all his spare time on mathematics, she joked that she wished he could teach her to add and subtract, which she was unable to do! Clearly finding a topic of mutual interest was not easy.

After this stay in hospital Grace spent some time convalescing in a nursing home. She disliked this change and her loss of independence. Writing to John Burke in August 1951, she gave a graphic account of all the reasons why she did not want to live permanently in a nursing home or guest house. Firstly, the meals were at fixed times and if she was late she would get nothing to eat. The main meal was usually at one o'clock and the tea or supper at five o'clock. This interval did not allow Grace enough time for visits to the city. Peak hour queues for public transport often forced her to stand for long periods in harsh winter weather. This tiring journey would be repeated if she went visiting or to a cinema in the evening. Grace also disliked the fact that she could not invite friends or relatives to have tea with her. Lastly, Grace felt that she could not live in one room as her artist's 'paraphernalia' was too extensive.

Grace gave up her flat in Nassau Street. Climbing the stairs there had become too much for her. She was anxious to find another place of her own and asked John Burke if he could make enquiries for something suitable. Her requirements were firmly stated. The hall door of the building must be open from 8 o'clock in the morning until 9 o'clock at night so that Grace would not have to go to the door for visitors or deliveries of milk and laundry. Secondly, the flat had to be self-contained to avoid leaving warm rooms for cold passages. Lastly, the flat should be at ground or first-floor level to avoid climbing too many stairs. In the same letter Grace told John Burke that she had 'completely run out of money' – a factor that made his task more difficult. Apartments in Dublin at that time were not as comfortable as they are today. Many of them were located in old houses that had not been properly converted. In general, the buildings had deteriorated since the days of their Georgian or Victorian grandeur as homes of well-to-do families. There were none of the modern comforts of central heating or double-glazing. However, John Burke, always a kind and patient friend to Grace, did his best to help her. Her shortage of money was partly due to medical expenses she had incurred. For the remainder of her life, Grace moved between apartments with periods spent in nursing homes. Sometimes she rented what John Burke regarded as substandard accommodation and he would help her to move to a better place.

In her last years Grace tried to continue her work. She had an idea that she might write stories for children and illustrate them herself. The manuscript of one story called *Koto the Great King* and several drawings survive[2] but nothing came of this project. Grace's poor health limited her capacity to work although she continued to sketch until the end of her life.

Illness took its toll on Grace in more ways than one. She became more demanding and at times was unreasonable with friends. Sadly, she quarrelled with Cathal Gannon who had been so good to her. Cathal had married in 1942. He was still working in Guinness' brewery where he put in a long day from 8 am to 5 pm. As a married man he was not available in the old way to visit Grace or do odd jobs, but she did not seem to understand this. She had been kind to Cathal's bride, Margaret Key, who stayed in Grace's flat several times before her marriage. As time passed Grace felt Cathal was neglecting her and eventually she wrote an angry letter of reproach to him. He wrote back, defending himself in detail, but it was of no use. In a final letter, posted on 5th January, 1953, Grace accused Cathal of selfishness and said she had been hurt by the way he had 'dropped' her.[3] By that time Grace's doctor told her that she had only a short time to live. She and Cathal did not meet again.

Grace died on 13th December, 1955 in an apartment at 52, South Richmond Street to which she had moved a short time before. She died suddenly and alone, a circumstance that saddened many people. A neighbour in the same house noticed on the evening of her death that Grace had not collected her post or milk bottle. The alarm was raised and when the flat was entered Grace was found lying dead in bed.[4] Relatives were informed and funeral arrangements were made. Her body was removed the next day to St Kevin's Church in Harrington Street, received by the Venerable Archdeacon Sherwin who also celebrated Requiem Mass the following morning. In 1916, he had received Grace into the Catholic Church in preparation for her marriage.

Attendance at the funeral was representative of many aspects of Grace's life. President Sean T. O'Kelly and his wife Phyllis, who had known Grace from youth, occupied special seats, as did Eamon de Valera. The chief mourners were Grace's three sisters – Nellie Donnelly, Katie Wilson and Sydney Czira – all of whom lived in Dublin. The younger generation included Grace's nephews, Donagh MacDonagh and Finian Czira, and her nieces, Maeve Donnelly and Helen Redmond. The Plunkett family was represented by Mr Jack Plunkett, Grace's brother-in-law, and his two sisters, Miss Fiona Plunkett and Mrs Geraldine Dillon. Politicians in attendance included Mr Sean MacBride, Dr James Ryan, Mr Oscar Traynor and Mr Harry Colley, all of whom were veterans of the War of Independence. Judge Cearbhall O'Dalaigh[5] was there with his colleague Judge Fawsitt. Other attendees included Mrs Nora Connolly O'Brien (daughter of James Connolly) and Mr Ronan Ceannt (the son of Eamon Ceannt). The Old Dublin Society was represented by its President Mrs Annie

Fraser. Others came as representatives of the trade union movement. Many former members of the old Irish Republican Army were also there. Grace's doctor, Eamon O'hOgain, came to pay his last respects.

Grace was buried with full military honours. Her coffin, draped with the tricolour, was laid to rest in the Plunkett family grave in Prospect Cemetery, Glasnevin. Prayers at the graveside were recited by four priests – the Reverend Eugene Nevin of Mount Argus, Father Basil of the Capuchins in Church Street, Father Fergal McGrath SJ and the Reverend Tomás O'Fiaich of Maynooth College.[6] The Irish Army provided a firing party and buglers, who played the final salute. Ann Burke who attended the Mass with her parents remembers Nellie Donnelly saying that she felt the military ceremonial was not altogether appropriate for her sister. Nonetheless Grace had become a powerful and symbolic figure of the republican ideal for which her husband had given his life. Her grave is situated close to the republican plot where famous fighters for Irish freedom are interred.

All the Irish newspapers noted Grace's passing, recalling the tragic circumstances of her marriage and her subsequent work as an artist. The *Irish Press* wrote that Orpen's portrait of Grace was prophetic, she *was* Young Ireland, gallant in her youth and staunch in her faith.[7] The most detailed appreciation came from the eloquent pen of Donagh MacDonagh in the same paper. He remembered hearing in his youth a ballad singer in Clare performing a song he had written about Grace:

> I loved Joe Plunkett and he loved me
> He gave his life to set Ireland free.

In this way Grace had entered what Donagh considered to be 'the most secure of all National Pantheons, the world of the ballad'. Her blonde beauty and slim figure had been admired in her youth, but Grace had wit and talent too. She would be remembered for all her personal qualities – especially her generosity – but inevitably such memories would only last for a time. Donagh concluded:

> What Ireland will remember longest is the scene at Kilmainham prison where she married, by the light of two guttering candles, the young man who was to be executed in a few hours. So she took her place with Sarah Curran in Ireland's romantic heart.

103

Now she is dead but as long as Ireland has a history she will be remembered.

This tribute says it all and leaves little for a biographer to add. Grace's art will always be there to showcase her talent and mirror the dramatic times through which she lived. More recently, a new ballad was written in memory of Grace and Joseph. The chorus runs as follows:

> Oh, Grace, just hold me in your arms
> and let this moment linger
> They'll take me out at dawn and I
> will die
> With all my love I'll place this wedding
> ring upon your finger
> There won't be time to share our love
> for we must say good-bye.[8]

Grace's gallantry was shown not only by her courage in 1916 but by the way she lived her life. At the time of her death, she had been a widow for thirty-nine years. No other man had touched her heart to the same extent as her young husband. How much her lively personality concealed will never be fully known. Grace was a reserved woman who seldom revealed her inner self. Her generation has now passed away and few remain who knew her well. Records remain of a unique life which will continue to fascinate other generations. Romantic Ireland is not yet 'dead and gone', contrary to the fears expressed by the poet, W. B. Yeats.

NOTES

1. I am grateful to Mrs Monica Henchy for this reminiscence.
2. In the author's possession, kindly donated by Ann Burke.
3. Cathal Gannon kindly gave me copies of his letter to Grace and her last letter to him.
4. Presumably the cause of death was heart failure. I have been unable to verify this as, due to some oversight, the death was not registered.
5. He later became Chief Justice and President of Ireland.

6. Later Cardinal Archbishop of Armagh.
7. Date was 14 December, 1955.
8. The ballad was popularised by the singer Jim McCann of The Dubliners group.

Bibliography

PRIMARY SOURCES

Papers of Grace Plunkett in the National Library of Ireland.
Papers of Josephine Plunkett in the National Library of Ireland.
Papers of Richard Mulcahy in the Archives of the National University of
  Ireland, Dublin.
"We Two Together" by James and Margaret Cousins.
Published in 1950 by Ganesh, Madras, India.
"The Years Flew By" by Sydney Gifford Czira (John Brennan)
Published in 1974 by Gifford and Craven, Dublin.
The Reminiscences of Cathal Gannon in the custody of Charles Gannon.
Joseph Holloway Papers in the National Library of Ireland.
Statement of Grace Plunkett for the Military History Bureau dated 1st.
  June 1949
Registry of Births Marriages and Deaths.
National Archives.

INTERVIEWS

Ann Burke
Maeve Donnelly
Charles Gannon
Monica Henchy
Professor Kevin B. Nowlan
Blanaid O'Brolchain
Eithne O'Byrne
Caithlin O'Neill
Oliver Snoddy

NEWSPAPERS AND PERIODICALS

Capuchin Annual 1942
Daily Sketch
Dublin Magazine Spring 1966
Eire 12th May 1923
Freeman's Journal
Homestead
Irish Booklover Volume 8 August - September 1916.
Irish Citizen
Irish Fun
Irish Independent
Irish Life
Irish Monthly Volume LXII April 1934
Irish Press
Irish Tatler and Sketch
Irish Times
Lloyd's Weekly News 7th May 1916
Studies 1917
University Review Volume I No. 12 1957

SECONDARY SOURCES

Bruce Arnold, *Orpen, Mirror to an Age*, Cape Publishers, London, 1981.
J. C. Beckett, *The Making of Modern Ireland*, Faber and Faber, London, 1966.
Henry Boylan, *Dictionary of Irish Biography*, Gill and Macmillan, Dublin, 1978.
Patricia Boylan, *All Cultivated People: a History of the United Arts Club, Dublin*, Colin Smythe, London, 1988.
Kathleen Clarke, *Revolutionary Woman*, O'Brien Press, Dublin, 1991.
Padraic Colum and others, *The Irish Rebellion of 1916 and its Martyrs* edited by Maurice Joy, New York, 1916.
Pat Cooke, *A History of Kilmainham Jail*, Stationery Office, Dublin, 1995
Anne Crookshank and the Knight of Glin, *The Painters of Ireland*, Barrie and Jenkins, London, 1978.
Seamus Deane and others, *The Field Day Anthology of Irish Writing* Volume 2, Field Day Publications, Derry, 1991.
Ruth Dudley Edwards, *Patrick Pearse: The Triumph of Failure*, Faber and Faber, London, 1977.
Elizabeth, Countess of Fingall, *Seventy Years Young* published in paperback by Lilliput Press, Dublin, 1991.
Desmond Fitzgerald, *The Memoirs of Desmond Fitzgerald*, Routledge and

Kegan Paul, London, 1968.

Christopher Fitzsimons, *The Boys*, Gill and Macmillan, Dublin, 1994.

R. M. Fox, *Rebel Irish Women*, Talbot Press Dublin, 1935.

— *History of the Irish Citizen Army*, Duffy and Co, Dublin, 1944.

Richard J. Hayes (ed.), *Sources for the History of Irish Civilisation 1940–1967*, Hall & Co. Boston, 1970.

Robert Hogan and Michael O'Neill (eds.), *Joseph Holloway's Abbey Theatre*, Southern Illinois University Press, 1967.

— *Joseph Holloway's Irish Theatre* Volume 2, Proscenium Press, Dixon, California, 1969.

Irish Times, *Sinn Féin Rebellion Handbooks* published in Dublin in 1916 and 1917.

Deidre Kelly, *Four Roads to Dublin*, O'Brien Press, Dublin, 1995.

Brendan Kennelly, *The Poetry of Joseph Plunkett* published in the Dublin Magazine Spring Issue 1966.

F. S. L. Lyons, *Ireland Since the Famine*, Weidenfeld and Nicholson, London, 1971.

Dorothy Macardle, *The Irish Republic*, Victor Gollancz, London, 1937.

Sinead McCoole, *Guns and Chiffon*, Stationery Office, Dublin, 1997.

Roger McHugh and Maurice Harman, *Anglo-Irish Literature*, Wolfhound Press, Dublin, 1982.

F. X. Martin (ed.), *Leaders and Men of the Easter Rising: Dublin 1916*, Methuen, London, 1967.

Brian Murphy, *Patrick Pearse and the Lost Republican Ideal*, James Duffy & Co. Dublin, 1991.

Liam O'Briain, *Cuimhri Cinn*, Sairseal and Dill, Dublin, 1974.

Leon O'Broin, *W. E.Wylie and the Irish Revolution*, Gill and Macmillan, Dublin, 1990.

Kit and Cyril O'Ceirin, *Women of Ireland: a Biographic Dictionary*, Tir Eolas, Kinvara, Co. Galway, 1996.

Ulick O'Connor, *A Terrible Beauty Is Born*, Hamish Hamilton, London, 1975.

Padraic O'Farrell, *Who's Who in the Irish War of Independence and Civil War 1916–1923*, Lilliput Press, Dublin, 1997.

Marie O'Neill, *From Parnell to De Valera: A Biography of Jennie Wyse Power 1858–1941*, Blackwater Press, Dublin, 1991.

Rosemary Owens, *Smashing Times*, Attic Press, Dublin, 1985.

Geraldine Plunkett (later Dillon), *University Review* Vol.1 Number 12. 1957.

—(ed.), *The Poems of Joseph Mary Plunkett*, Talbot Press, Dublin, 1917 (includes portrait by Mrs Joseph Plunkett).

Joseph Mary Plunkett, *The Circle and the Sword*, Maunsel & Co. Dublin, 1911.

Theo Snoddy, *Dictionary of Irish Artists*, Wolfhound Press, Dublin, 1996.

Walter Starkie, *Scholars and Gipsies*, John Murray, London, 1963.
John Turpin, *A School of Art in Dublin since the Eighteenth Century*, Gill and Macmillan, Dublin, 1995.
Katherine Tynan, *The Years of the Shadow*, Constable, London, 1919.
Caitlin Bean Ui Thallamhain, *An Pictuir Ar An mBalla*, Clodhanna Teoranta, Dublin, 1973.
Margaret Ward, *Unmanageable Revolutionaries*, Brandon Press, Dingle, Co. Kerry, 1983.
— , *Hanna Sheehy Skeffington*, Attic Press, Cork, 1997.
Robert Welch, *The Oxford Companion to Irish Literature*, Clarendon Press, Oxford, 1996.

Index